NOBODY'S COMING TO SAVE YOU

BY MELVIN JOHNSON

Acknowledgments I want to thank everyone who has supported my journey in writing this book. Your encouragement, belief, and feedback have made this project possible. To my family, friends, and supporters— this book is for you.

CONTENTS

Preface - This book wasn't written from a place of perfection. It wasn't born out of a polished strategy or a textbook understanding of life. It was written out of survival. Out of pain. Out of years spent waiting for something—or someone—to come and change everything for me.

I spent a lot of time in the struggle. Real struggle. Not the kind you post about online for sympathy, but the kind that eats at your confidence, your identity, and your hope. There were moments when I felt invisible, like no matter how hard I worked, nobody would ever recognize my value. Moments when I sat in silence wondering if this was all life had for me.

But the truth hit me like a punch in the chest: **nobody was coming to save me**. Not my family. Not my friends. Not some magical opportunity. If I wanted to change my life, I had to become my own rescue.

This book is for anyone who's ever felt stuck, forgotten, underestimated, or behind. It's not a feel-good collection of clichés. It's a blueprint for those who are ready to own their power and stop waiting for permission to rise.

You'll read about mindset. You'll see stories—some personal, some imagined—that hold up a mirror to your choices. You'll feel uncomfortable at times. That's good. Growth isn't always pretty, but it's always necessary.

If you made it to this page, something inside of you already knows what needs to happen. You're not looking for a savior. You're looking for a strategy, a spark, and a reminder that you're more powerful than you've been led to believe. This is that reminder.
Let's begin. — *Melvin Johnson*

Chapter 1

The Foundation of Self-Reliance

The journey toward personal and professional success starts with one fundamental truth: nobody's coming to save you. No one is going to hand you success, wealth, happiness, or fulfillment. If you want it, you have to go and take it. That's what self-reliance is—understanding that you are the architect of your own life, the builder of your own future. No matter where you come from, what cards you were dealt, or what obstacles stand in your way, the moment you take full responsibility for your life, you unlock the power to change it.

My Personal Wake-Up Call

I remember exactly when this lesson first hit me. I was about twenty years old, working for the Claire McCaskill Campaign for Governor of Missouri. My friends and I dedicated ourselves to this campaign, pouring months of effort into it. We traveled from city to city, knocking on doors, speaking to residents, and pushing hard to help McCaskill win. We believed in what we were doing, and more importantly, we believed that all our work would be rewarded.

We were promised that at the end of the campaign, we would be adequately compensated for our efforts. They even gave us rental cars to use freely for the duration of those four to five months. We were young, hungry, and willing to do whatever it took to prove ourselves. We had this belief that if we just put in the work, if we just showed up every day and gave it everything we had, things would fall into place for us.

But then the campaign ended. Claire McCaskill didn't win. And suddenly, all of the promises meant nothing. We were told to drop off the vehicles, turn in our campaign materials, and that was it. No compensation. No follow-up. No "thank you" for all the hard work. Nothing.

That moment was my first real taste of reality. I realized that it doesn't matter how hard you work sometimes. It doesn't matter how much effort you pour into something. If you're waiting for someone to take care of you, waiting for someone to save you, you're setting yourself up for disappointment.

I had genuinely believed that the people I worked for were going to help me in some way. That they would see my effort and offer me a job or open a door for me. But that wasn't the case. It wasn't Claire McCaskill herself who let us down—it was the system around her, the campaign managers, the people who made the promises but never followed through.

I was young, and it hit me hard. But looking back, that experience was one of the most valuable lessons I ever learned. Because from that moment on, I stopped waiting. I stopped believing that hard work alone would be enough. I realized that if I wanted a future, I had to build it myself. I had to take control, to stop depending on people who had no real stake in my success, and to make sure I was never in that position again.

That was my wake-up call. And it's the same wake-up call I'm giving you now.

Defining Self-Reliance

Self-reliance is not about simply working hard or having confidence. It's about knowing that if everything in your life crumbles, you will not crumble with it. It's about developing the ability to stand tall when the ground beneath you shakes, when the people you trust disappear, when the institutions that are supposed to protect you fail. What do you do when you have no safety net? Do you fall, or do you rise?

This is not a hypothetical question. For many people, the world has proven time and time again that it is unreliable. Parents abandon their children. Friends betray trust. Governments pass laws that fail to protect the people they claim to serve. Jobs disappear overnight. Spouses leave. Tragedy strikes. What then? If your entire sense of stability is built on external forces, you are setting yourself up for devastation. Because at some point whether it's today, tomorrow, or years from now something will happen that shakes your world.

Self-reliance means understanding that while you may not be able to control what happens around you, you can always control how you respond. You can either collapse under the weight of hardship, or you can learn to navigate it. You can either wait for someone to come along and fix things for you, or you can figure out how to fix them yourself. And once you learn how to do that, you become unbreakable.

Relying on yourself doesn't mean shutting people out or refusing help. It means knowing that if help never comes, you'll still find a way forward. It means developing the mental toughness to stand alone if necessary, to push forward without needing permission, and to trust yourself more than you trust the unpredictable world around you.

Some people see this as a burden. I see it as the greatest gift you can give yourself. Because the moment you stop expecting the world to save you, you gain the power to save yourself. And that power? That power is freedom.

Real-Life Example: Tyler Perry's Journey

Tyler Perry is one of the most powerful figures in entertainment today, but his journey to success wasn't easy. He grew up in a household filled with abuse, struggled with homelessness, and faced rejection after rejection. Most people would have given up. But Perry refused to let his circumstances dictate his future.

In 1990, he moved to Atlanta and used his savings to produce his first play. It was a complete failure. He lost everything. But instead of quitting, he kept pushing, refining his craft, and reinvesting in himself. For six years, he worked tirelessly, living in his car at times, until finally, one of his plays broke through.

That moment of success wasn't luck—it was the result of relentless self-reliance. Today, Perry is a billionaire, owning one of the largest film studios in the world, built on land where his ancestors were once enslaved. His story proves that no matter where you start, if you refuse to quit, success is inevitable.

Setting the Stage for What's to Come

This book isn't just a collection of motivational words—it's a blueprint for transformation. Over the next fifteen chapters, we're going to break down exactly what you need to know, understand, and execute to fully embrace self-reliance. We're not just talking about financial independence, mindset shifts, or goal setting—we're going deeper. We're going to dismantle the mental, emotional, and

social conditioning that has kept you stuck. We're going to address the reasons why you may have spent years waiting for someone to give you permission to move forward. And more importantly, we're going to replace those patterns with new, actionable ways to take control of your life.

Each chapter will focus on a critical aspect of self-reliance, from rewiring the beliefs that were ingrained in you as a child, to positioning yourself in a way that guarantees success, to understanding the science behind resilience and why failure isn't the enemy—it's the best teacher you'll ever have. We'll explore financial strategies, communication techniques, and even the psychology behind influence, ensuring that by the time

you reach the last page; you will have every tool necessary to take control of your own life.

But make no mistake—this isn't easy. This book will challenge you. It will force you to confront hard truths, to look at yourself in ways you may have been avoiding. Some of the ideas here may make you uncomfortable, but that's the point. Growth doesn't happen in comfort zones.

By the end of this book, you won't just understand self-reliance—you'll embody it. You'll no longer be waiting for opportunities; you'll be creating them. You won't be hoping for change; you'll be making it happen. And most importantly, you'll stop believing the lie that someone, somewhere, is coming to make your life easier.

Because the truth is, nobody is coming to save you. And that's the best news you'll ever hear.

Chapter 2

The Mirror of Self-Reflection

In the pursuit of personal growth and success, the journey begins with self-reflection. Just as a sculptor must understand the block of marble before carving a masterpiece, you must first understand yourself to shape your future. Self-reflection is the cornerstone of transformation, the moment where dreams begin to crystallize into tangible goals.

The Power of Self-Reflection

Every achievement starts with a clear vision. Self-reflection isn't just an exercise; it's a powerful psychological tool. It forces you to step back, strip away distractions, and examine who you really are, what you truly desire, and what's holding you back. Without this process, you're wandering through life reacting rather than strategizing.

Why Self-Reflection Matters

Most people go through life without questioning their choices, their habits, or even their desires. They follow routines, chase goals society has placed upon them, and never stop to ask themselves if this is truly what they want.

Self-reflection provides emotional stability by allowing you to understand your triggers, fears, and motivations, helping you make decisions from a place of clarity rather than reaction. It develops self-awareness, helping you recognize and leverage your strengths while working on your weaknesses.

It improves decision-making by aligning choices with personal values and goals instead of impulse or external pressure. It enhances influence, making communication, leadership, and relationships more effective.

Without self-reflection, you risk living on autopilot, following paths that may not serve you. The most successful individuals don't leave their lives to chance; they deliberately evaluate, adjust, and grow with intention.

Defining Your Path

Are You Moving with Purpose or Just Moving?

Imagine getting in a car and driving without a destination. You'll end up somewhere, but will it be where you truly want to go? Life operates in the same way. Without self-reflection, you risk chasing empty goals, pouring energy into unfulfilling pursuits, and wasting years moving in the wrong direction.

What do you truly want? Not what your family expects. Not what society dictates. What do you, deep down, want for your life? Many people never ask themselves this question seriously. They chase jobs, relationships, and lifestyles that don't align with their authentic desires, only to find themselves unfulfilled years later.

The key is to pause and reflect. Ask yourself what excites you, what you would pursue if money weren't an issue, when you feel most alive, and what dreams you've been putting off. These questions uncover the desires that matter most to you.

Creating a Strategic Plan

Once clarity is gained, the next step is crafting a structured plan to achieve it. A goal without a plan is just a wish. Wishing leads nowhere—consistent, intentional action is what turns visions into reality.

A structured approach brings vague dreams into focus. It begins with defining a specific goal, whether it's building a successful business, writing a book, or mastering a skill. It requires an understanding of what you're willing to sacrifice—whether it be time, energy, comfort, or old habits—to make that goal a reality.

Setting a deadline creates urgency and focus. A definite plan, broken into clear steps, provides a roadmap to follow. Writing this plan as a clear, concise statement solidifies your commitment. Reading that statement daily keeps the vision fresh in your mind, reinforcing your dedication to achieving it.

Real-Life Example: My Weight Loss Journey

To illustrate the power of setting a goal and following a structured plan, consider my weight loss journey.

Imagine I was at 380 pounds, and I set a goal to lose weight and improve my health. I didn't just say, "I want to lose weight." I created a plan:

Daily non-negotiables:

Walk 10,000 steps every day. Drink 45 ounces of raw fruit juice. And progressively increase physical activity.

Gradual Adjustments: Start with small dietary changes instead of extreme diets that are impossible to maintain.

Tracking Progress: Monitor weight, energy levels, and body measurements weekly.

Accountability: Check in with a coach or use a journal to stay consistent.

Commitment to the Long Game:

I Understood that real transformation takes time and for me it took over 16 months to be able to look in the mirror and like what I see.

But the real lesson isn't just about weight loss—it's about commitment to a structured plan, even when motivation fades. The hardest days, the ones where quitting feels like the easiest option, are the days that define your success.

This transformation didn't happen overnight, and it certainly wasn't easy. There were days filled with frustration, moments of self-doubt, and times when the scale didn't move. But through persistence, consistency, and unwavering commitment to the process, the goal was achieved.

My weight loss journey mirrors any personal transformation. Whether your goal is financial independence, career success, or mastering a skill, the same principles apply. Progress is slow, but consistency leads to results. Small, daily habits create massive, long-term change. Excuses will always be there—discipline is choosing action over comfort.

The result? Over 160 pounds lost. Not because of luck, but because of consistent, disciplined action aligned with a structured plan. This approach works for anything in life, not just health. Success, in any form, follows the same formula: Set a goal, build a plan, commit to the process, and stay the course—even when it's hard.

Breaking the Habit of Self-Deception

Self-reflection requires brutal honesty. Many people deceive themselves into thinking they're putting in the work when they're actually making excuses. They say they want success, but their actions tell a different story.

Someone may claim they want financial freedom yet fail to track their expenses or reduce unnecessary spending. Another may insist they want to be in better shape, yet avoid consistent workouts, choosing convenience over commitment. A writer may dream of finishing a book but find endless distractions rather than sitting down to write.

Self-deception is one of the biggest barriers to success. It's easier to justify inaction than to admit when we aren't doing enough. The mind excels at crafting rationalizations—convincing you that you're waiting for the right time, that you're doing all you can. But is that true?

The people who succeed in life are the ones who break free from their own excuses. They identify patterns of procrastination, avoidance, and distraction. They stop lying to themselves and take full accountability for their progress—or lack thereof.

Self-Reflection in a Crisis

True self-reflection is tested in moments of hardship. When things fall apart—whether it's financial struggles, job loss, personal betrayal, or a health crisis—that's when reflection becomes crucial.

Instead of blaming external forces, successful individuals ask themselves the hard questions. What role did I play in this situation? What lesson can I take from this hardship? How can I grow stronger because of this?

A crisis reveals the truth about a person. It forces them to confront their weaknesses, insecurities, and fears. But it also presents an opportunity—to rebuild, to evolve, and to erge stronger. Those who crumble do so because they resist reflection. Those who rise do so because they adapt, recalibrate, and move forward with intention.

Practical Exercises for Self-Reflection

One of the most effective ways to practice self-reflection is through journaling. Taking time each morning or evening to write about what moved you toward your goals, and what you could have done better, creates a habit of accountability. The five-why exercise helps uncover true motivations—by repeatedly asking "why" behind a goal, you get to the root of your drive.

Creating a vision board keeps your aspirations in clear view, reminding you daily of what you are working toward. Silent reflection allows for uninterrupted contemplation—ten minutes each day spent in silence, free from distractions, provides clarity. Regular accountability checks keep you honest. By evaluating actions each week and asking if you truly followed through, you reinforce a commitment to growth.

Conclusion: Aligning Your Path with Your Vision

Self-reflection isn't a one-time exercise—it's a lifelong commitment. It keeps you aligned with your vision, helps you adjust your course, and ensures that you move with purpose rather than drift aimlessly.

In the face of setbacks, the unreflective person sees only failure, while the reflective person sees an opportunity. The difference is perspective. If you want to create the life you envision, you must be ruthlessly honest with yourself, acknowledge your shortcomings, and commit to growth.

Now, the challenge is on you. Take time to sit in silence today. Ask yourself the hard questions. Define the steps that align with your vision. Nobody's coming to save you—but with self-reflection, you'll realize you never needed anyone to.

Chapter 3

Embracing Financial Self-Reliance

Understanding the Stakes

Money isn't just about numbers—it's about freedom, security, and control over your life. But here's the harsh truth: no one is going to rescue you from financial struggle. No magic windfall is coming. No government program, no rich relatives, and no stroke of luck will replace what you must do for yourself. If you don't take charge of your financial destiny, you're handing over control to circumstances, to employers, to luck. And luck is a terrible financial strategy.

Yet so many people hesitate. They avoid looking at their bank statements, procrastinate on planning for the future, or push money decisions aside because it feels overwhelming. Maybe they think they'll get serious about it 'later.' But here's the thing—later has a way of turning into never.

The cost of inaction is real. One day, you wake up and realize you've spent decades trading time for money, with nothing to show for it but an endless cycle of bills and debt. If you don't take control now, the future won't wait for you to be ready.

Think of the person who has spent twenty years at a job they hate, earning just enough to cover rent, utilities, and groceries. Every month is the same—just barely getting by, waiting for that raise, that promotion, that break. But it never comes. And when they finally stop to look back, they realize something chilling: they've been running on a hamster wheel, moving but going nowhere.

Now picture someone else—same job, same salary, but a different mindset. Instead of waiting for a raise, they create their own financial plan. They start investing small amounts, cutting out unnecessary expenses, and learning about money. In twenty years, they've built a safety net, an investment portfolio, and choices. They may still be working, but they're not trapped. They have options. And options mean freedom.

Which one will you be?

Facing Financial Fears

Why do so many people avoid confronting their finances? Fear. Fear of realizing they've wasted too much time. Fear of acknowledging how little they actually have saved. Fear that they might have to change their habits—and let's be honest, change is uncomfortable.

But fear is more than just discomfort. It's deeply rooted in psychological and generational conditioning. Many people were raised in environments where money was a source of stress rather than a tool for security. If you grew up watching your parents struggle, argue about bills, or live paycheck to paycheck, that becomes your default understanding of money. Whether you realize it or not, those early experiences shape your financial behaviors today.

Some people avoid looking at their finances because they fear confirming their worst assumptions. They don't want to see how much debt they have, how little they've saved, or how far behind they are. But avoidance doesn't change reality—it just delays the inevitable. And the longer you avoid it, the bigger the problem becomes. That's why debt snowballs. That's why financial anxiety keeps people up at night. And that's why some people stay trapped in a cycle of poverty, passing those fears down to their children.

But here's the truth: facing financial fears is the first step toward breaking generational curses. Financial instability is often inherited, not because of genetics, but because of habits, mindsets, and a lack of education. If no one in your family has ever built wealth, it might seem impossible. But just because it hasn't been done before doesn't mean it can't be done now. Someone in the family has to be the first to break the cycle. Why not you?

Think about what happens when one person in a family decides to take control of their finances. They start learning about credit, investing, budgeting, and building assets. They pass that knowledge down to their children. Instead of growing up in fear of money, the next

generation grows up understanding how to use it. They see wealth as something achievable, not just for 'other people.' They inherit knowledge, not just bills. And knowledge is the foundation of generational wealth.

Generational wealth isn't just about leaving behind a pile of money. It's about passing down a mindset—a way of thinking about money that empowers future generations. It's teaching your kids how to manage money, so they never have to struggle like you did. It's creating a legacy where financial security is the norm, not the exception.

But it all starts with one decision: to stop running from money and start mastering it. The moment you take control; you change your family's future. You become the one who shifts the narrative. You stop reacting to money with fear and start using it as a tool for freedom. And when you do that, you give your children, and their children, a different reality.

Now ask yourself: Are you willing to do what it takes to be the first in your family to break the cycle? Or will you let fear keep you stuck in the same struggles that have trapped generations before you?

The Psychology of Money

People think wealth is built by making huge, dramatic financial moves—winning the lottery, getting a massive salary, stumbling upon a business idea that changes everything overnight. That's a fantasy. The reality is that financial security and wealth are built quietly, consistently, over time. It's about habits, discipline, and a mindset shift.

Money is emotional. It's tied to our upbringing, our experiences, and even our sense of self-worth. Some people believe they're 'bad with money' because that's what they were told growing up. Others develop spending habits as a form of emotional comfort—buying things to feel successful, to fill a void, or to keep up appearances. These psychological patterns run deep, and unless they're addressed, they keep people stuck.

One of the biggest psychological traps is *instant gratification.* It's the reason people choose a new car over investing, an expensive vacation over saving, or dining out every night instead of cooking at home. The human brain is wired to prioritize immediate rewards, which is why long-term financial planning feels difficult. But successful people learn to override this impulse.

They understand that small sacrifices today lead to massive rewards in the future.

Another critical mindset shift is moving from a *scarcity mentality* to an *abundance mentality.* People with a scarcity mindset believe there's never enough—they hold onto money tightly, avoid investing, and fear taking risks. Those with an abundance mindset understand that money is a tool that can grow when used wisely. They see opportunities instead of limitations. They take calculated risks and make money work for them instead of living in constant fear of losing it.

Think about this: If you suddenly received $10,000, what would you do? Someone with a scarcity mindset might stash it away out of fear, while someone with an instant gratification tendency might spend it immediately. But a financially disciplined person with an abundance mindset would find a way to invest that money and turn it into more.

Wealth isn't just about numbers in a bank account. It's about changing how you *think* about money. It's about breaking free from self-sabotaging behaviors and building habits that lead to long-term success. And most importantly, it's about recognizing that financial freedom isn't a fantasy—it's a series of small, intentional choices made consistently over time.

The Story of Arkad: Wealth in Babylon

Thousands of years ago, in the city of Babylon, there was a man named Arkad. He wasn't born into wealth. In fact, he started out as a simple scribe—no riches, no privilege, just a desire for more. He could have accepted his circumstances. But instead, he learned the secrets of wealth from the wise and applied them with discipline.

Arkad's journey didn't start with success. It started with curiosity and humility. He sought out the wealthiest man in Babylon and asked the simplest but most important question: *How did you become wealthy?* The answer wasn't about luck or inheritance—it was about discipline, patience, and a mindset shift.

The principles Arkad followed were simple:

Save at least 10% of every dollar you earn. Before you spend on luxuries, entertainment, or even essentials, pay yourself first. This habit ensures that no matter how much you make, you're always building wealth.

Live below your means. Arkad understood that wealth isn't about income—it's about how much you keep. He resisted the temptation to increase his lifestyle as his earnings grew, choosing instead to reinvest in his future.

Make your money work for you. He didn't let his savings sit idle. Instead, he sought out opportunities to invest wisely, allowing his wealth to multiply over time.

Guard your investments. Many people lose wealth faster than they build it by chasing quick profits or trusting the wrong people. Arkad was careful with his money, ensuring that his investments were sound.

Continue learning. Financial wisdom isn't a one-time lesson—it's a lifelong journey. Arkad kept seeking knowledge, refining his strategies, and teaching others what he learned.

Arkad didn't just amass wealth for himself; he shared his knowledge, helping others in Babylon rise out of financial struggle. His wisdom became a cornerstone for those who wanted to break free from the cycle of poverty.

What makes Arkad's story powerful is its timelessness. The same principles that worked thousands of years ago still apply today. The methods might change—investing in stocks, real estate, or businesses instead of gold or trade—but the core philosophy remains the same: consistent, disciplined financial habits lead to lasting wealth.

So, ask yourself: Will you apply these principles to your own life? Will you be the Arkad of your generation? The one who shifts the financial future of your family? The one who turns struggle into security, uncertainty into confidence?

The choice is yours. The knowledge is available. The opportunity is now. The only thing left to do is start.

A Tale of Two Investors

Let's talk about two friends: Marcus and Jordan.

Both started working at 18, earning similar wages. Marcus, after getting advice from an older mentor, decided to start investing just $20 a week into a simple S&P 500 index fund. Not a lot. Just the cost of a couple of fast-food meals or a few drinks at the bar.

Jordan, on the other hand, thought, *What difference does $20 make?* So he spent it instead—on entertainment, eating out, random impulse buys.

Fast forward 30 years. Marcus has built a six-figure investment portfolio. Just by consistently investing $20 per week, letting compound interest do its thing, and

staying disciplined, he's now looking at over $100,000 in investments. If he continues, he'll be set for life by retirement.

Jordan? He's saved nothing. He's worked just as hard as Marcus, but he has nothing to show for it financially. He's still living paycheck to paycheck, waiting for something—anything—to change.

Marcus' wealth wasn't built by luck. It wasn't built by genius-level investing skills. It was built by simple, consistent action over time.

But let's take this a step further. What if Marcus, instead of just investing $20 a week, found ways to gradually increase his contributions? What if he took advantage of employer-matching retirement accounts? What if he used bonuses, tax refunds, or side hustle income to grow his investments even further? His six-figure portfolio could easily turn into millions by the time he retires.

Meanwhile, Jordan's financial habits keep him trapped. As the years pass, his expenses increase. He takes out loans to cover emergencies. He never builds an emergency fund, so every unexpected bill throws him further into debt. And when retirement approaches, he realizes he has no savings, no assets, and no plan.

This isn't just a hypothetical scenario—it's reality for millions of people. Many assume that wealth is out of reach because they don't make six figures, but the truth is, wealth isn't about how much you earn—it's about what you do with what you have.

Imagine if Jordan had made just one change early on redirecting that $20 from impulse spending to investing. The trajectory of his entire life would have been different. That's the power of small, intentional financial decisions.

The lesson here is simple: Wealth is built through discipline and time, not luck. It's not about massive windfalls or sudden riches—it's about consistency. The earlier you start, the better, but even if you feel like you're late, taking action now is better than never starting at all.

So, ask yourself:

Are you making your money work for you, or are you letting it slip through your fingers?

Are you choosing temporary comforts over long-term security?
Are you willing to shift your mindset and take responsibility for your financial future?

Because in the end, the difference between Marcus and Jordan isn't intelligence, background, or luck. It's one simple decision: the decision to invest in the future instead of just living for today.

So again, ask yourself: are you going to be Marcus or Jordan?

Why Financial Independence Matters

People associate wealth with luxury—the cars, the houses, the vacations. But that's not real wealth. Real wealth is having control over your life. It's the ability to walk away from a toxic job. It's knowing that if an emergency happens, you're prepared. It's waking up in the morning and choosing what you want to do with your day—not being forced into it because of financial desperation.

Wealth isn't about looking rich. It's about freedom.

So many people wake up every day and trade their time for money. They work jobs they hate, answering to people they don't respect, because they have no other choice. But if you build financial independence, you take back control. You decide how you spend your time. And time is the most valuable asset you'll ever have.

Think about this: What if money were no longer a deciding factor in your daily life? What if your bills were covered, your savings were growing, and you no longer had to make decisions out of necessity but out of choice? That's what financial independence provides—the power of choice. It's the difference between living reactively and living proactively.

The true cost of financial dependence isn't just struggling to pay the bills. It's being stuck in unhealthy relationships because you can't afford to leave. It's staying in a stressful job because you have no backup plan. It's postponing your dreams, putting off experiences, and watching life pass by because your finances won't allow you to take risks.

Financial independence gives you the power to reclaim your time. Imagine waking up and choosing to spend the day however you want—working on passion projects, traveling, spending time with family, or simply enjoying life. That's what wealth is. Not the material things, but the control over your most valuable asset: your time.

Achieving financial independence isn't about making millions overnight. It's about taking deliberate steps—saving consistently, investing wisely, and learning to make your money work for you. The earlier you start; the sooner you can reclaim your time and stop letting money dictate your life.

Here's the reality: The system isn't designed for you to be financially free. It's built to keep you dependent—on paychecks, on debt, on jobs you don't like. But once you realize this, you can break free. You can create a plan, build assets, and take control.

So, the real question is: How long are you willing to trade your time for money before you start making money work for you?

Breaking Free from the Paycheck-to-Paycheck Cycle

If you feel like you're constantly just scraping by, that's not an accident. The system is designed to keep you dependent, to make sure you're always in just enough debt, always working just enough to keep the lights on but never enough to break free. The moment you realize this, you can begin the process of breaking out of the cycle.

It starts with awareness. Most people have no real idea where their money is going. They work hard but see their paychecks vanish before the month is over. Bills, expenses, debts, and unnecessary spending drain their income faster than they can replenish it. When you start paying attention—truly examining how you spend—you gain control over your financial reality. Awareness forces you to ask the hard questions: Is this expense necessary? Am I spending money that could be put toward financial growth? Is my money working for me, or am I just working for money?

Breaking free also requires discipline. Cutting unnecessary expenses doesn't mean living like a monk, but it does mean making better choices. Do you need to eat out five times a week, or could you cook at home and put that money into savings? Do you really need the latest phone upgrade, or would that money be better spent in an investment account? Small, intentional shifts create long-term results.

And then there's the most important shift: mindset. Moving from a consumer to an investor mindset changes everything. Instead of thinking, *how can I spend this money?* You start asking, *how can this money work for me?* That's the difference between those who stay trapped in the paycheck-to-paycheck cycle and those who break free. Every dollar you earn is an opportunity—not just to pay bills, but to create financial stability and wealth.

Most people won't take these steps. They'll keep waiting for the right moment, making excuses, telling themselves they'll start next year. But next year turns into the year after that. And then another. And before they know it, decades have passed, and nothing has changed.

But the few who take control? They change their lives forever.

The Real Question

So here's what it comes down to: Where do you see yourself in five years? Are you going to be in the same financial position, still struggling, still waiting for the perfect moment to take action? Are you going to keep putting off the decisions that could change your life, telling yourself you'll start tomorrow, next year, or when circumstances improve?

Or are you going to start now—today—and take control of your financial future? Because here's the truth:

Nobody's coming to save you. There's no magic moment, no perfect set of conditions, no rescue plan that will do the work for you. But that's not bad news—it's the best news you could ever hear. Because it means *you* have the power. You don't have to wait for permission. You don't have to hope for a lucky break. You get to make the decisions that shape your future.

Financial freedom isn't about waiting for the right opportunity. It's about creating it. It's about taking small, consistent steps, even when it feels like progress is slow. It's about making choices that your future self will thank you for—whether that's skipping a purchase today so you can invest in your future or learning to think differently about money, so you never feel powerless again.

The hard truth is that most people won't take action. They'll read this, agree with it, feel inspired for a moment, and then go back to their routine. But the ones who do take action? They will change their lives forever. They will look back five years from now and realize they're in control, not just surviving but thriving.

So ask yourself: Will you be the person who keeps waiting? Or will you be the one who takes control? Because the choice is yours. Your future self is depending on you. The only question left is: *What are you going to do about it?*

Chapter 4

Breaking Free from the Mental Trap

Have you ever had that restless night, staring at the ceiling, asking yourself why your life isn't what you dreamed it would be? You might push that thought aside, burying it beneath daily routines or distractions. Yet, deep down, you know that question holds the key to your fulfillment.

We often avoid it because confronting it means facing uncomfortable truths. It means acknowledging that the reason you're not where you want to be isn't due to luck or circumstance—it's you. That realization can be terrifying, but it's also the most liberating truth.

This chapter's purpose is to rattle you awake, to force you to see the real reasons your life isn't where you want it to be. Once you confront these truths, hiding behind excuses won't be an option anymore, and that's when real change begins.

If you're not living your best life, it's time to face the mirror and ask: **why?**

The Lie You've Been Sold

From the moment we're born, we're conditioned to believe that happiness, security, and success come from external sources.

Think about it—how many times have you been told that a good job will take care of you? That your family will always have your back, no matter what? That the government is there to protect you, or that faith alone will provide?

These messages are often comforting, but they can also lull us into a false sense of security, making us believe that our future lies in the hands of others.

But here's the hard truth: Nobody is coming to save you. It's not that people don't care—it's that they're all wrapped up in their own battles, struggling to keep their own heads above water.

And while you're waiting for that perfect moment, the ideal circumstance, or someone else's permission, life keeps moving.

Years slip by, and suddenly, you find yourself wondering why nothing has changed. But the moment you stop waiting and start acting, that's when life shifts.

Confronting the Barriers in Your Mind

Imagine standing at the foot of a mountain, staring up at its peak. The climb seems impossible, not because you lack the strength or gear, but because you've convinced yourself you can't do it.

This mountain isn't made of rock or snow—it's built from your beliefs, fears, and excuses. It's the invisible chains that hold you back from reaching your potential. To climb this mountain, you must first confront these barriers.

Your upbringing. The beliefs your family and environment instilled in you. Think about the messages you absorbed as a child. Maybe you were told that certain dreams were "unrealistic," or that people like you don't

achieve certain things. If these beliefs aren't questioned, they become walls between you and your potential.

Your fears. The fear of failure, rejection, or not being good enough. It's natural to fear the unknown, but staying in the same place out of fear isn't safety—it's stagnation.

Your excuses. The stories you tell yourself to justify why you can't move forward. These excuses may feel real, but they're often just comfortable narratives that keep you in your comfort zone.

To break free, you have to recognize these barriers and actively dismantle them. Only then can you start climbing that mountain.

The Beliefs You Inherited

Consider the beliefs you grew up with. Perhaps your parents told you to play it safe, that aiming too high would lead to disappointment. These messages, often given with good intentions, can unknowingly become self-imposed limitations.

But those beliefs aren't immutable laws; they're just narratives handed down through generations.

Think about the voice in your head telling you that you can't achieve certain things. Whose voice is it? A parent? A teacher? Society? Recognizing this is the first step to reclaiming your own story.

Challenge these inherited beliefs. Just because something was true for those who came before you doesn't mean it has to be true for you. The power to redefine your life lies within your ability to challenge what you've been taught and write a new narrative.

The Fear of Change

Change is daunting because it often feels like stepping into the unknown. Your brain, hardwired for survival, equates the familiar with safety—even if that familiar is a situation that's limiting or harmful.

Consider why people stay in jobs they hate or relationships that drain them. It's not because they're unaware of the possibilities beyond—it's because the brain sees any deviation from the norm as a potential threat.

But in reality, staying in a comfort zone out of fear isn't preserving safety—it's preserving stagnation. To break this pattern, you have to confront the fear head-on and recognize that growth lies on the other side of discomfort.

The Stories You Tell Yourself

The most damaging lies aren't the ones others tell you—they're the ones you repeat to yourself. These are the stories that become your reality, shaping your actions and limiting your potential.

Consider the times you've told yourself, "I don't have time," while spending hours on social media. Or when you said, "I don't have the money," but managed to find cash for non-essentials. These narratives feel real because they're familiar, but they're ultimately just stories.

Rewriting these stories is within your power. When you start seeing excuses for what they are—self-imposed barriers—you can begin to dismantle them and pave the way for real change.

The Cost of Staying Stuck

Imagine fast-forwarding five years into the future. If you don't make a change now, where will you be? Often, the answer is unsettlingly clear: in the same job, facing the same struggles, feeling the same frustrations.

The truth is, if you don't act, you remain stagnant. And that stagnation is often more costly than any risk you might take. By not making a change, you're choosing to miss out on the potential of a more fulfilling life, and that decision comes with its own price.

The only way to alter your future is by taking responsibility for the present. It might be uncomfortable, but it's the only way to break the cycle.

The Shift: From Wanting to Needing

There's a profound difference between wanting something and needing it. Wanting is a passive state—a longing for a better future that may never arrive. Needing, however, is a relentless drive to make that future happen.

When you shift from wanting change to needing it, you ignite a fire within you. You stop waiting for the stars to align and start aligning them yourself. You move from dreaming to doing, from planning to executing.

We'll dive deeper into this concept in Chapter 12, but for now, understand that shifting your mindset from wanting to needing is where real transformation begins.

The Breaking Point

Every transformative journey has a moment of reckoning—a breaking point where enough is enough. It's that pivotal moment when the discomfort of staying the same outweighs the fear of change. For some, it's a sudden realization; for others, it's a gradual build-up that finally reaches a tipping point.

If you haven't reached that breaking point yet, you can manufacture it. It starts with a decision—a conscious choice to draw a line in the sand and refuse to settle for less than you deserve.

This is the moment you stop playing small, stop settling, and start stepping into the person you were meant to be.

Final Question: Are You Willing to Change?

By now, you're standing at a crossroads. One path leads back to life as usual, filled with familiar excuses and unfulfilled dreams. The other path—less traveled but infinitely more rewarding—demands that you take control, let go of excuses, and step boldly into action.

The choice is yours, and it starts now. You don't need external validation or someone else's permission to begin. The realization that you are the only one responsible for your future is both liberating and empowering.

So, what are you going to do? This is the moment you decide whether you stay in the comfort of the known or step into the vast potential of the unknown. **Nobody's coming to save you—but you don't need them to, because you have everything you need within you.**

Chapter 5

Positioning Yourself for Real Change

Most people don't fail because they lack talent or intelligence. They fail because they never position themselves for success. They might have ambition, desire, and even knowledge, but without placing themselves in the right environment,

mindset, or structure, they struggle to execute change. The difference between those who succeed and those who don't isn't luck—it's positioning.

This chapter explores what it means to position yourself for meaningful and lasting transformation, whether in your career, finances, relationships, or personal development. If you're not strategically placing yourself in situations that promote success, you're actively placing yourself in situations that don't.

Why Most People Never Change

Have you ever felt stuck, like no matter how much effort you put in, nothing seems to change? If you've tried to improve your life, whether it's losing weight, making more money, or enhancing your mindset, you've likely hit a wall. The reason is simple: wanting change isn't enough. If wanting were enough, everyone would already be living their dream lives. Success isn't just about desire; it's about positioning yourself so that success becomes inevitable.

Your environment, habits, and mindset play critical roles in this. If you don't position yourself in a way that supports your goals, you will fail—no matter how much you want it. Many people believe success is about working harder, but in reality, it's about working smarter structuring your life so that success becomes the natural outcome.

The Power of Positioning in the World

When you look at the most successful people in any field, you'll see a common thread: they didn't rely solely on talent or effort. They positioned themselves in a way that made their success unavoidable. Apple positioned itself as the premium tech brand, so customers expect innovation and exclusivity. Oprah Winfrey positioned

herself as the voice of personal development, so people see her as an authority. Certain politicians position themselves as "for the people" or "for change," regardless of their actual policies.

Positioning isn't just about being the best—it's about being perceived in a way that makes success automatic. This concept applies to individuals as much as it does to brands. If you don't position yourself for success, someone else will shape how the world sees you.

Step 1: Control Your Environment

You are a reflection of the people, ideas, and habits you surround yourself with. If you spend time with people who complain and see the world through a lens of negativity, you'll find yourself adopting their mindset. Conversely, if you surround yourself with action-takers who are building wealth and improving themselves, you'll naturally elevate to their level. Napoleon Hill called this the Mastermind Principle—the idea that your success is directly tied to the people you associate with.

Your environment isn't just about people—it's also the content you consume, the habits you reinforce, and the beliefs you absorb. What you watch, listen to, and read all shape your reality. If you want to position yourself for success, flood your environment with things that align with your goals.

Step 2: Build Systems, Not Just Motivation

Motivation is a fleeting force. It's like a spark that ignites but quickly fades. Successful people understand this, which is why they don't rely on motivation alone. Instead, they build systems—structured routines that make success automatic. James Clear, in Atomic Habits, emphasizes that real success comes from small, consistent improvements, not drastic, overnight changes.

Building a system means creating an environment where the right choices happen naturally. This could mean removing obstacles that prevent positive habits, attaching new habits to existing ones, and celebrating small wins along the way. The goal is to create a structure where the right choices become second nature.

Step 3: Adopt an Identity-Based Mindset

Your identity is your greatest weapon in making change. If you still see yourself as someone who struggles or "isn't good at" something, you'll never reach the next level. It's not just about setting goals—it's about seeing yourself as the kind of person who naturally achieves those goals.

For instance, shifting from a goal-based mindset of "I want to be rich" to an identity-based mindset of "I am a person who builds wealth" changes how you approach every decision. If you see yourself as an athlete, you'll take care of your body without a second thought. Positioning yourself starts with how you see yourself and transforming that identity into reality.

Step 4: Stop Tolerating Mediocrity

Most people tolerate mediocrity because it's comfortable. They might not like where they are, but they're comfortable enough to stay there. They say they want more, but they choose immediate comfort over long-term progress. They might want financial freedom, but they spend money on things that don't build wealth.

Until your standard changes, nothing else will. You have to demand more from yourself than anyone else ever will, refusing to settle for anything less than what you deserve.

Your Future is Your Choice

Positioning yourself for success is about more than setting goals—it's about making deliberate choices that align with your vision. This means consciously creating an environment that fosters growth, building systems that ensure consistent progress, and adopting an identity that reflects the person you aspire to be.

When you raise your standards and refuse to settle for mediocrity, success becomes a natural extension of who you are. The individuals who achieve greatness aren't inherently more talented; they simply position themselves better.

So, ask yourself: Are you setting yourself up for inevitable success? The path you choose today will shape your tomorrow.

The Question You Must Ask Yourself

The individuals who succeed in life aren't always the smartest or the strongest—they're the ones who intentionally position themselves to win. So, the real question isn't whether you have the potential to succeed—it's whether you're placing yourself in the right environments, with the right people, and within the right structures to make success inevitable.

Every choice you make and every action you take either moves you closer to your goals or keeps you where you are. Your future is shaped by the decisions you make today, and by consciously choosing to position yourself for success, you take control of your narrative.

Chapter 6

The Resilience Blueprint – Turning Setbacks into Strength

If you're afraid of failure, it's not the failure itself you fear—it's the misconception of what failure means. Most people see failure as a verdict—a judgment that they're not good enough, smart enough, or capable enough. Each misstep feels like a reflection of their worth. But in reality, failure isn't an identity—it's feedback. It's a signpost showing you where to go next.

Science, history, and human experience all converge on this truth: failure isn't the opposite of success—it's the prerequisite for it.

This chapter will shatter the myth of failure and give you the tools to reframe every setback as a steppingstone to greatness. When you realize that failure is the most essential part of success, every misstep transforms from a roadblock into a lesson, guiding you towards your ultimate goal.

The Science Behind Failure and Learning

People often view failure as a signal to stop, a confirmation that they're heading in the wrong direction. But science paints a different picture.

Neuroscientists studying how humans learn have discovered that the brain actually **strengthens when it encounters failure**. Each mistake corrected reinforces neural pathways, making them more resilient. This process builds pattern recognition, allowing your brain to adapt, adjust, and improve based on past experiences.

The takeaway is clear: **the more you fail, the more equipped you become to succeed.** Those who experience multiple failures are often better prepared for eventual success. Failure isn't a detour; **it's the foundation of mastery.**

Case Study: The Growth Mindset Experiment

In a well-known study by psychologist Carol Dweck, students were presented with difficult puzzles. One group was praised for their intelligence: "You're so smart!" The other group was praised for their effort: "You worked really hard on that!"

When faced with harder challenges, the students praised for their intelligence hesitated. They avoided difficult problems to protect their image of being "smart." In contrast, the students praised for their effort embraced the challenge, viewing each obstacle as an opportunity to grow.

The takeaway is powerful: **if you see failure as a judgment of who you are, you'll avoid risks. But if you see failure as a tool for learning, you'll thrive.**

Reframing Failure: The Power of Perspective

Failure isn't something that happens to you; **it's something that happens for you.** The way you interpret setbacks determines whether you grow or quit. Imagine two people starting a business: both fail within the first year. One sees it as proof they're not cut out for success and gives up. The other studies what went wrong, makes adjustments, and tries again, ultimately finding more success in the next attempt.

The difference isn't the event—it's the interpretation. Your perspective on failure shapes your future. Embracing failure as a learning opportunity rather than a personal indictment opens the door to growth and resilience.

Embracing the "Failure = Data" Mindset

Failures aren't personal; they're data points that guide your next move. When a business venture doesn't pan out, it's not a reflection of your worth. It's feedback on what didn't work. By analyzing what went wrong, you gain insights that shape your future strategies.

Instead of seeing failure as a setback, view it as a necessary step in your journey. Each experience— whether success or failure—adds a layer of knowledge, making you more prepared for what comes next.

When things don't go as planned, approach them with curiosity rather than self-judgment. Consider each setback an opportunity for a "post-failure debrief."

Reflect on what happened: What exactly went wrong? What factors contributed to it? What can you learn from this? And what will you do differently next time? By treating setbacks as data, you strip away the emotional weight, allowing yourself to grow with each experience.

Building Resilience Through Repetition

Success often comes down to persistence—the willingness to keep going, even when faced with repeated failures. The more attempts you make, the more you learn and refine your approach.

Consider the "10,000 Experiment Rule"—a concept that suggests mastery is built through continuous trial and error. The best performers, whether in chess, sports, or business, don't achieve greatness by avoiding mistakes— they embrace each failure as a critical part of the learning process, building resilience through repetition.

The "Fail More, Fear Less" Challenge

The best way to overcome the fear of failure is to confront it head-on. Imagine intentionally setting out to fail at something every day for a week. Ask for a discount and face rejection, try a new skill and be terrible at it, pitch an idea and get turned down.

The point isn't the failure itself but the realization that failure is a part of life. Each time you fail, you'll find that the sting of rejection lessens, and you become more resilient. The more you normalize failure, the less you fear it—and the more unstoppable you become.

Study the Failures of the Greats

History's most successful individuals weren't immune to failure—they simply endured more of it than others.

Thomas Edison famously failed thousands of times before perfecting the lightbulb. Michael Jordan missed over 9,000 shots and lost nearly 300 games. Oprah Winfrey was fired from her first television job for being "unfit for TV."

Their stories aren't about overcoming impossible odds but about embracing failure as an integral part of success. Their resilience turned setbacks into stepping stones. They weren't inherently special—they were relentless.

The Only True Failure is Giving Up

At the end of the day, the only way to truly fail is to stop trying. Every mistake, setback, and loss is just a lesson in disguise. When you view failure as a stepping stone rather than a dead end, you unlock the potential to transform setbacks into strengths. Resilience isn't about avoiding failure—it's about using it to fuel your journey forward.

A Shift in Perspective: What's Coming Next

Up until now, *Nobody's Coming to Save You* has been a deep dive into self-reliance, mindset shifts, and the raw truth about taking control of your life. You've been challenged, confronted with tough realities, and hopefully, inspired to take action.

But now, **everything is about to change.**

Chapters 7 through 9 will take you on an entirely different journey—a **fictional yet deeply symbolic horror story**. This story is not just for entertainment. It is designed to **test the very principles you've been learning in this book**.

You will be introduced to **Sheriff Caleb Thornton and Mason Carter**, two characters who find themselves in a terrifying battle against an unknown force. They are faced with danger, uncertainty, and the looming realization that—just like in real life—**nobody is coming to save them**.

Why This Matters

This story is meant to be an **experience**, not just a break from the nonfiction insights you've been absorbing. It will challenge you to think about:

✓ **How fear impacts decision-making.**

 ✓ **What happens when people ignore warning signs.**

 ✓ **How survival and success require the same mental discipline.**

 ✓ **How resilience is the ultimate deciding factor between those who make it and those who don't.**

By the end of Chapter 9, you'll see how **this story connects directly to the real-world lessons in this book**. When you return to the nonfiction portion, you'll come back with a **new perspective**, a deeper emotional connection, and a greater understanding of why self-reliance is not just an option—it's a necessity.

A Final Warning...

This section will pull you in. It will test you. And when it's over, you may never look at fear, self-doubt, or personal responsibility the same way again.

So, take a deep breath And let's begin.

Chapter 7

The Town That Forgot Its Ghosts

Black Hollow was the kind of town that felt frozen in time, untouched by the rush of the world beyond its borders. Nestled deep in the backwoods, where the roads twisted like veins through an aging body, it was a place where people still locked their doors at sundown and whispered about things they pretended not to believe in. The town had a way of swallowing its history, burying its ghosts beneath layers of silence and tradition.

Sheriff Caleb Thornton knew this better than anyone.

He had spent his entire life in Black Hollow—first as a boy racing through the fields, then as a man carrying a badge. The town was in his blood. So were its stories.

*Some of those stories had faded over time, becoming nothing more than hushed warnings passed between generations. But the legend of **Black Hollow House** never died.*

Every generation had its own version of the tale— accounts of strange figures at the windows, of shadows moving when no one was there, of children vanishing

without a trace. The house loomed at the edge of town, forgotten by time but never truly gone.

Caleb had always told himself those were just stories.

Until the disappearances started again.

Three people in the last year alone. A drifter passing through town. A teenager who dared his friends to go inside. And most recently—Elijah Carter. That one had been different. Elijah wasn't some outsider or reckless kid. He was one of them. Someone Caleb had known since they were kids.

The town had moved on quickly. Black Hollow always did. The disappearances became whispers and then silence. The people who had lived here long enough knew better than to ask questions. Some things were best left alone.

*But **Mason Carter** wasn't like the others.*

He refused to let the town forget.

Now, standing in Caleb's office, he was demanding answers.

"You're not just going to let this go," Mason said, his voice edged with frustration. "Not this time."

Caleb leaned back in his chair, studying him. The kid had his brother's fire, but none of his caution. "What do you want me to do?" Caleb asked. "Send a team in to chase ghosts?"

Mason's jaw tightened. His fists clenched at his sides. "I'm going in there," he said.

*Caleb exhaled slowly. He had spent years keeping people from making **stupid** decisions. But Mason's mind was already made up.*

And deep down, Caleb knew the truth.

The town had ignored Black Hollow House for too long. "If you're going," Caleb said, standing, "I'm going with you." Mason blinked, as if he hadn't expected Caleb to say yes. But it was already settled. The house had waited long enough.

Chapter 8

Into the Dark

*The air **changed** the moment they stepped onto the property.*

Caleb felt it immediately—a weight pressing against his chest, thick and suffocating. It wasn't just the damp scent of rotting wood or the overgrown weeds swallowing the porch. It was something deeper, something wrong.

The house was waiting for them.

*Mason pushed forward, his boots crunching against the brittle leaves littering the steps. He didn't hesitate. Caleb did. Not out of fear—at least, not the kind he could name—but because every instinct told him this was a **bad idea**.*

Still, he followed.

The front door groaned as Mason shoved it open, revealing an entrance swallowed by darkness. Caleb's flashlight sliced through the black, illuminating dust dancing in the stale air.

The house should have felt empty. It didn't.

*The space seemed to **breathe** around them. The floorboards creaked under their weight, the air thick with something **damp** and **rotting**.*

Caleb's grip tightened on the handle of his service weapon. "You sure about this?"

Mason didn't answer. He stepped forward, his gaze scanning the room like he was looking for something. Or someone.

*Caleb followed, his eyes flicking to the **covered furniture**. White sheets draped over old chairs and tables, but it felt less like protection from dust and more like they were **hiding something**.*

*Then the **whisper** came. So soft it barely existed. A sound at the edge of his hearing. Caleb froze. His breath hitched. "Did you hear that?" Mason gave a slow nod. His voice was quiet but steady. "It knows we're here." A* *chill crept up Caleb's spine. He didn't ask Mason what it was. He didn't want to know.*

*They moved deeper into the house, their flashlights barely cutting through the thick blackness swallowing the hallway. The second floor smelled of mildew and something else—something sickly and **stale**, like air that had been trapped for decades.*

Caleb's stomach churned. He hated this.

*Every part of him screamed to **turn around**, to **get out** before it was too late. But Mason had that look—the one that said they weren't leaving until he got answers.*

*They stepped into what had once been a bedroom. The broken curtains let in just enough moonlight to cast **jagged shadows** across the walls.*

Then Caleb saw them.

*Scattered across the wooden floor—**old, yellowed papers**.*

He knelt, picking one up.

*It was **handwritten**. Crude. Desperate.*

The ink had bled into the paper over time, but the words still clawed their way through.

It watches from the walls. It feeds when we fear. We tried to leave. We never could.

A cold knot tightened in Caleb's stomach. "Mason..."
But Mason wasn't listening.

He was staring at something across the room—a mirror, cracked and leaning against the wall.

Caleb followed his gaze.
Something was wrong with the reflection.

Mason's flashlight beam trembled across the glass, distorting the fractures, but that wasn't what made Caleb's breath hitch.

His own reflection was staring back at him. But it wasn't moving the same way he was. The whisper came again.
Louder this time.

A voice that wasn't theirs.
"Don't look away."

Caleb ripped his gaze from the mirror and grabbed Mason's arm. "We need to go."

Mason didn't move.
His hand was pressed against the glass, his fingers **trembling**.

"It's here," he whispered.
*Then the **light flickered**.*
*The air turned **ice cold**.*
*And the **whisper laughed**.*

Chapter 9

The Fight or the Fall

*The whisper turned into **laughter**.*

Low at first, curling through the dark like a breath against Caleb's neck. Then it grew—twisting, stretching, filling the room until the walls themselves seemed to vibrate with it.

*The mirror **shuddered**.*
Mason's fingers twitched against the glass. His breath came in shallow gasps,

*his body **frozen** in place.*
*Caleb **acted without thinking**. He grabbed Mason's arm and yanked him back just as the **mirror crack'd wider**, splitting like a wound.*

*A **hand**—long, gnarled fingers **too dark, too thin**— pushed from the reflection. It didn't reach out so much as* *it bled from the glass, stretching unnaturally into the room, its shape never quite settling.*

*The laughter **stopped**.*
*A silence followed, thick and **waiting**. Then Mason **screamed**.*

*His body **arched backward**, his limbs seizing as if something **inside him was being pulled away**. His eyes went **white**, his mouth opening wide, but no sound came out now—just a **guttural, suffocating choke**.*

*Caleb **didn't hesitate**.*

*He lunged forward, wrapping his arms around Mason and yanking him free from whatever unseen force had taken hold. The air turned **solid**, like thick, pressing tar, fighting against him.*

*He reached for his weapon—instinct, habit—but somehow he **knew** a bullet wouldn't stop this.*

*His eyes **darted to the broken mirror**, to the **jagged shards** scattered across the floor.*

*The whisper had come from the mirror. The **laughter, the thing, the presence—it was inside the glass.***

Caleb didn't think.

He **grabbed a shard**—*its edge slicing into his palm*—and **drove it into the figure's reaching hand.**

The reaction was **instantaneous**.

The **room howled**—*not a sound, but a force, something deep and guttural that cracked through the walls and splintered the floor beneath them. The figure **jerked backward**, recoiling, the glass flickering as though **something had been severed**.*

Mason **collapsed**.

Caleb grabbed him, **dragging him toward the door** *as the house **groaned around them**. The walls trembled, dust **raining from the ceiling**, the entire structure **shrinking in on itself**.*

They **ran**. *Caleb didn't look back. He didn't want to see what was behind them.*

The moment they **crossed the threshold**, *the house **exhaled a** deep, sucking pull that sent them both **tumbling into the dirt** as the front door **slammed shut behind them**.*

*Silence. Only the sound of their **breathing**, ragged and uneven.*

*Mason coughed, his hands gripping the damp earth as if trying to convince himself it was real. **He was real.***

*Caleb pushed himself up onto his knees, his chest heaving. The weight that had been pressing against him since the moment they arrived was **gone**. The house— whatever it was, whatever had been inside it—was **silent.***

*Mason wiped a shaking hand across his face. Then he **laughed.***

*It wasn't joyful. It wasn't a relief. It was the sound of **someone who had survived something they were never meant to escape.** Caleb let out a slow breath. He **understood.***

*They sat there for a long moment, staring at the house, waiting for something—**anything**—to happen.*

Nothing did. Caleb turned to Mason. "It's over."

*Mason shook his head, **eyes still locked on the house**. "You sure?"*

*Caleb didn't answer right away. The presence that had haunted them, that had **owned them**, was gone. **But was it ever really over?***

He looked at Mason, then back at the house. "It has to be."

Mason let out another breath. Then he nodded. "You were right," he said quietly. "No one was ever coming."

Caleb's jaw clenched.
No one had ever come to save them.
*But they **didn't need anyone**.*
*They had **saved themselves.***

Chapter 10:

The Road Nobody Expected Me to Walk

A Shift in Perspective

You've just experienced a story that wasn't merely about fear—it was about **what fear represents**. That horror story wasn't just fiction. It was a **mirror** reflecting the doubts and insecurities that haunt us all.

For some, fear takes the shape of shadows in an old house, something unseen watching from the dark. But for most of us, fear is much closer. It's the weight of uncertainty, the feeling of being trapped in a place you don't belong, the belief that if you take a step forward, something might pull you back.

The creature in the mirror isn't just a monster—it's the reflection of doubt, hesitation, and every voice that's ever told you **can't**.

But here's the truth:

Fear is only as powerful as you allow it to be. It's a narrative that can either hold you back or propel you forward. The real horror story isn't about the monster in the dark. It's about letting that fear dictate your life.

But I didn't let it win. And that's why we're here.

Fighting for My Future

Most people don't know this, but my father was a professional boxer—a **world champion**. But by the time we met at my college graduation, I had already learned to fight my own battles.

Growing up in **Kansas City, Missouri**, was a lesson in survival. **Drugs. Violence. Broken families.** The chaos wasn't an abstract threat—it was the reality I woke up to every day. The streets don't care about your dreams; they remind you of where you come from every chance they get.

When a fight broke out between me and some neighborhood guys, it wasn't just a schoolyard scuffle—

it was serious. It was enough for my mother to pull me out of high school entirely. That moment could have defined me.

But it didn't.

Instead, I enrolled myself in another school. I was determined to finish, no matter what. But the environment didn't change. Violence was still a constant presence, lurking around every corner. So, when I got caught with a weapon at school, I wasn't using it or threatening anyone, but it didn't matter. I was removed from school again.

That could have been the moment I gave up. But I didn't. Despite being removed, I still had enough credits to graduate. Even though I wouldn't walk the stage with my classmates, I knew that **graduation wasn't the real finish line.**

This moment was about more than a diploma—it was about defying the narrative that had been written for me. I refused to let my circumstances dictate my story. Instead, I took control of my own future.

Chasing Something Bigger

After high school, I did what many people do when they're searching for a way out—I turned to **music**.

I became a rapper, known as **Mel Balu**, and quickly found local success. People started recognizing my name, and for a while, it felt like I had found a way to break free from the world I grew up in. Music was my escape, my way of turning the chaos into something meaningful.

But I quickly learned that music is a gamble. It's a world where you can pour your heart into every lyric and still face the uncertainty of never breaking through. The fleeting nature of the industry made me realize that I needed something more stable—something that would allow me to have real control over my future.

That's when I got into the nightclub business. I co-founded **Club Sweat**, and this time, I hit it big. The club was a massive success, drawing in crowds and giving me a sense of accomplishment I'd never felt before.

But even as I built that success, I realized I wasn't done yet. There was a part of me that still craved more—not just more success, but more control over my own destiny.

The Hardest Decision of My Life

At some point, I had to ask myself a question that would change everything: **Do I stay in Kansas City and keep doing what I'm doing, or do I take a chance on something bigger?**

It was more than a decision about geography. It was about **leaving behind everything I knew**—my businesses, my comfort, my reputation. But most painfully, it meant leaving behind my **oldest children**.

That decision broke me in ways I didn't think were possible. Every instinct told me to stay, to be there for them, to keep them close. But deep down, I knew that if I wanted to create the life, I envisioned for them, I had to go.

Leaving Kansas City wasn't abandoning them—it was about building something **for them**. I had to trust that they'd understand, even if it took years for them to see the bigger picture.

We stayed connected, with them visiting every summer and holiday. And now, we're closer than ever, but when I first left, I didn't have that certainty. I only had a vision and a gut feeling that I was doing the right thing.

No one was there to tell me it was okay. No one could see the bigger picture except me. But I knew that sometimes, the hardest decisions are the ones that carve the path to the future we dream of.

Nobody Is Going to Tell You It's Okay

When you make **hard decisions**, when you **take risks**, when you **bet on yourself**—there's often no one there to reassure you. Nobody will hold your hand or validate your choices. The journey to success, to building the life you envision, is often lonely.

Most people won't understand your decisions until years later, when they see the results. Even then, some will still think it was luck, not recognizing the sacrifices and risks that brought you here.

But that's the reality of forging your own path. It's about having the courage to see beyond the present, to trust your vision even when no one else can.

The Truth About Taking Control

Everything I've built—every single thing—has been the result of me making the decision to do what nobody expected me to do.

I wasn't supposed to graduate. I wasn't supposed to succeed in business. I wasn't supposed to make it out of Kansas City. And I sure as hell wasn't supposed to be writing this book.

But I did it anyway. And I didn't wait for anyone to tell me it was okay. That's the real difference between people who stay stuck and people who move forward. The ones who move forward don't sit around waiting for permission. They just go. They make the hard choices, they take the risks, and they own every single mistake along the way.

Owning Your Story

This book isn't an autobiography. I'm not just sharing my story for the sake of it. I'm sharing it because I know you have your own battles to fight. Maybe you've been told you won't make it, that the

obstacles are too big, or that the setbacks are insurmountable. But your story isn't written yet. **Nobody is coming to save you,** and that's not a bad thing. It means you have the power to be your own hero, to shape your own destiny.

No one else will see the bigger picture like you do, and that's your advantage. Stop waiting for someone to give you permission. Stop looking for validation. The only person who can truly give you that is yourself. **Go.**

Chapter 11

The Power of Your Circle – Who's in Your Corner?

If there's one thing I've learned on this journey, it's this: you cannot do it alone.

Yes, self-reliance is the foundation of success, but success itself is not a solo mission. The people you surround yourself with will either push you forward or pull you back.

Your circle is more than just your friends, co-workers, or family—it's the people who influence your thoughts, your decisions, and your energy. If you spend your time with small thinkers, complainers, and people who accept mediocrity, it won't be long before you start doing the same. But if you position yourself among **visionaries**,

action-takers, and problem-solvers, your mindset and results will shift.

The truth is your circle will **make** or **break you.**

Most people stay stuck because they're surrounded by the wrong people. They spend their time with individuals who reinforce their fears, keep them tethered to their past, and discourage them from taking risks. It's not always intentional—sometimes, it comes from the people who claim to love you the most. The ones who tell you to be realistic, to stay safe, to not reach too far beyond what you've always known. But if you want to elevate your life, you need to audit your circle and build one that challenges and inspires you.

The people around you shape your beliefs, your energy, and your opportunities. The right people push you forward. The wrong people keep you stagnant.

A Story of Betrayal and Blindness

History is full of people with talent, ambition, and vision who failed—not because they weren't good enough, but because they surrounded themselves with the wrong people.

Julius Caesar was one of the most brilliant and ambitious leaders of all time. He reshaped Rome, expanded its empire, and built a reputation that made him both revered and feared. His influence was unmatched. But despite his military genius and political mastery, he made one fatal mistake—he trusted the wrong people.

As Caesar's power grew, so did his list of enemies. The Roman Senate feared what he had become. They whispered in dark chambers, warning that he sought to make himself king—something Rome had vowed never to allow again. His popularity among the common people was a threat to the elites who wanted to hold onto their own power. They began to conspire against him, plotting in secret.

But among all his enemies, one betrayal cut deeper than any other.

Marcus Junius Brutus was not just another senator. He was someone Caesar considered a friend, a man he had mentored and believed in. Again and again, Caesar defended Brutus from accusations of disloyalty, convinced that Brutus would never turn against him. Despite the warnings, despite the growing unrest, Caesar refused to believe that the people closest to him would be the ones to take him down.

He ignored the signs.

On the morning of March 15, 44 B.C., Caesar walked into the Senate chamber, unaware that his circle had already sealed his fate. The betrayal was swift. The knives came without hesitation. And in his final moments, as he lay bleeding on the marble floor, he saw the face of the one man he had trusted Brutus.

Legend says his last words were: *"Et tu, Brute?"* Not just words of shock, but of deep, soul-crushing betrayal.

The very person he thought would stand beside him had delivered the final blow.

But this wasn't just about Caesar. Brutus, too, had surrounded himself with the wrong people. He let the voices of his conspirators sway him. He allowed fear,

jealousy, and pressure to convince him that turning on Caesar was the right move.

And what did it bring him? Chaos.

Brutus and the other assassins thought they had saved Rome, but in reality, they had only doomed themselves. Caesar's loyalists launched a brutal campaign of revenge. Within months, Brutus was hunted down, abandoned, and alone.

His final moment was not one of triumph—it was one of regret.

The lesson is clear. Caesar fell because he ignored the warnings about his circle. Brutus fell because he let the wrong people shape his decisions.

Both men were brilliant. Both had power. Both had potential for greatness. But neither survived because neither built the right circle around them.

Who's in Your Corner?

The people around you are either sharpening you or dulling you. There is no in-between.

Some will challenge you, inspire you, and push you to be your best. Others will subtly discourage you, tell you what you can't do, or hold you back—sometimes without even realizing they're doing it.

If you look at the people closest to you and don't feel challenged, motivated, or encouraged, you have a problem.

Not everyone deserves access to you. Not everyone should be allowed into your inner circle.

The people around you should be driven, solution-oriented, and action-takers—the kind of people who don't just talk about success but actually do the work. The kind of people who uplift you, not weigh you down.

If someone is constantly negative, doubting, or pulling you back, they do not belong in your circle.

Changing your circle isn't easy. It can be uncomfortable. It might mean distancing yourself from old friends, limiting your time with certain family members, or stepping into new, unfamiliar environments.

But if you want to level up, you need to be in the right rooms.

Opportunities don't just happen—they come from the right people, in the right places, at the right time. The biggest deals, the most valuable partnerships, and the most life-changing conversations don't come from job boards or chance—they come from who you know.

The Shift That Changes Everything

No matter where you are in life right now, you can start making changes. You don't need to be rich or successful to shift your environment. All it takes is being intentional about who you allow into your space.

This is where most people get it wrong. They think success is about talent or hard work alone. But the truth is, it's about positioning. It's about who you listen to, who you learn from, and who you allow to influence your mindset.

The people in your circle will either accelerate your success or ensure that you stay exactly where you are.

Take a hard look at your relationships. Are the people in your life pushing you forward, or are they holding you back?

Because success isn't just about what you do—it's about who you do it with.

If you want to change your life, change your circle.

Start curating your environment. Surround yourself with people who challenge and inspire you.

And watch how fast your life transforms. Because no one is coming to save you.

But the right people will push you to save yourself.

Chapter 12

The Fire That Fuels Success – The Power of Desire

If there's one undeniable truth that separates those who succeed from those who don't, it's desire. Not hope. Not wishful thinking. Not passive dreaming. Desire. A fire so strong that it refuses to be ignored, a hunger that turns every obstacle into fuel, a force that bends reality to its will.

Napoleon Hill laid it out in *Think and Grow Rich*—that all success begins with an intense, burning desire. But most people fail before they even start because they don't understand the difference between wanting something and needing it.

That difference is everything.

The Divide Between Want and Need

Most people go through life wanting things. They want more money. They want a better job. They want to be in shape. But the truth is, wanting is weak. Wanting is passive. Wanting is saying, "It would be nice if this happened."

A must-have is different. A must-have is non-negotiable. It's something you refuse to live without. It's the air you breathe.

Imagine someone holding your head underwater. In that moment, do you *want* air? Or do you *need* it? Do you casually hope to breathe, or do you thrash, kick, claw, and fight with everything in you until you pull oxygen into your lungs?

That's what real desire feels like.

That's the kind of energy you need to bring to your goals.

Most people don't reach their potential because they don't operate with that level of urgency. They treat their dreams like a casual preference, not like something their survival depends on.

But the people who make history? The ones who reshape industries, redefine possibilities, and leave legacies?

They treat their vision like oxygen.

A Story That Changed Everything

Before I truly understood the power of desire, I was like most people. I had goals, but I wasn't attacking them with urgency. That changed the day I read *The 48 Laws of Power* by Robert Greene.

One story in particular shook me to my core—the story of Louis XIV, the Sun King.

Louis wasn't born into absolute power. As a young prince, he was surrounded by men who held the real control—powerful ministers who dictated how the government ran, who made the decisions while he simply wore the title of king.

Most people in his position would have accepted it. They would have settled for the comfortable life of royalty without responsibility. But Louis had a fire inside him that wouldn't let him accept being a figurehead.

His desire wasn't just to rule. He wanted absolute power.

So, he studied. He observed. He waited—not passively, but strategically, like a predator waiting for the perfect moment to strike.

When the time came, he took control with ruthless precision. He stripped the nobility of their influence, centralized all power in himself, and built the Palace of Versailles—a symbol not just of wealth, but of dominance. He ruled France with complete authority for over seventy years, shaping it into one of the most powerful nations in history.

That story changed me. It made me question myself in ways I hadn't before.

I wanted success, but was I obsessed with it? Was I willing to restructure my entire life around it? Was I treating it like oxygen?

That moment of self-reflection marked the beginning of a shift. And I never looked back.

The Fatal Weakness of Those Who Lack Desire

For every Louis XIV, for every person who bends the world to their will through sheer determination, there's someone else—someone with all the talent, all the intelligence, all the potential—who never makes it.

One of the most painful examples in history is Nikola Tesla.

Tesla was a genius. His mind operated on a level so advanced that even today, many of his ideas remain beyond what's possible. He was a visionary, an inventor, a scientist whose work could have redefined human progress.

But Tesla had a fatal flaw.

He lacked the ruthless, unwavering desire to see his vision through—at least not in the way that would have secured his place in history during his lifetime.

Compare him to Thomas Edison.

Edison was not Tesla's equal in intelligence. His inventions weren't as groundbreaking. He wasn't a genius in the way Tesla was. But Edison was relentless.

When he set out to create the light bulb, he failed over 10,000 times. And yet, he kept going.

Tesla, at one point, worked for Edison. He had ideas that could have revolutionized electricity forever, but he made a fatal assumption—that his brilliance alone was enough.

Tesla expected the world to recognize his genius. He expected people to come to him, to fund his ideas, to reward him for thinking at a higher level.

Edison didn't wait for permission. He fought. He built. He marketed. He sold his vision with the energy of a man who needed to win.

And in the end, Edison built an empire.

Tesla died broke, alone, and forgotten—until history redeemed him decades too late.

Tesla wanted to change the world.

Edison had to.

That's the difference. That's the only difference.

Do You Have Real Desire?

Let's start with the truth. Most people don't have real desire.

They think they do. They convince themselves they want something badly. But when faced with sacrifice, when forced to make hard choices, they hesitate. They wait. They make excuses.

Desire isn't just a feeling—it's a force.

The word *desire* comes from the Latin *desiderare*, which means "to long for, to await with deep intensity." But real desire is even more than that. It is an unshakable, all consuming force that pulls you toward what you must have, regardless of obstacles.

Desire is the refusal to accept anything less than what you are chasing.

If you truly desire something, you will rearrange your entire life to get it. Not "try." Not "hope." Not "someday." You will move mountains. You will change everything. You will keep pushing—no matter how long it takes, no matter how hard it gets.

That's what separates those who succeed from those who stay stuck.

But here's the real question: Do you actually have desire?

Or are you lying to yourself?

If you say you want something, but you aren't obsessed with it, you don't have desire.

If you say you want something, but your actions don't reflect it, you don't have desire.

If you say you want something, but you haven't sacrificed for it, you don't have desire.

You just have a wish.

And here's the truth—wishes don't change lives. Desire does.

So let's put it to the test.

The Desire Challenge

You say you have desire. You say you want success. You say you're hungry for more.

Let's find out if that's true.
For the next seven days, I want you to prove it.

1. Eliminate one major distraction that is stealing your time—TV, social media, gaming, mindless scrolling.

2. Wake up one hour earlier every day and use that time to work on your goal.

3. Do one thing every day that moves closer to what you claim you want.

No matter how small, you must take action.

Most people won't do this. They'll read it, agree with it, and then do nothing.

Will you be one of them? Or will you prove to yourself that your desire is real?

Because at the end of the day, desire is not proven through words—it's proven through action.

If you can't commit to seven days of action, you don't have real desire. You have a fantasy.

So decide. Right now. Do you have desire? Or are you just pretending?

What Comes Next

Now that you understand the power of desire, it's time to apply it.

The next chapter is about translating that fire into action—taking the steps that separate the dreamers from the doers.

Because at the end of the day, desire without action is just fantasy.

Chapter 13

The Art of Mastering Communication – Unlocking Influence

Imagine stepping into a room with nothing—no connections, no wealth, no formal advantages. Just your presence, your words, and your ability to capture attention. And within minutes, the entire room is listening. Not just hearing you but believing you. Trusting you. Feeling compelled to follow you.

This is the power of communication.

It is the difference between being overlooked and being unforgettable. Between being ignored and being a force of nature. The ability to speak in a way that moves

people, that shifts perspectives, that creates urgency—
this is not just a skill. It is the single most valuable
weapon in the arsenal of every great leader, entrepreneur,
and visionary in history.

Few people embodied this power more than Jordan
Belfort, the infamous Wolf of Wall Street. His ethics may
have been questionable, but his ability to influence was
undeniable.

Belfort didn't just sell stocks—he sold belief. He
understood something that most people never grasp
people don't make decisions based on logic. They make
decisions based on emotion.

Numbers didn't matter. Financial reports didn't matter.
What mattered was the feeling he created. When he
spoke, he painted a vision so vivid that people could see
it, taste it, feel it. He gave them certainty when they had
doubts, confidence when they hesitated. He moved
them—not with information, but with raw, undeniable
conviction.

That is the art of communication.

Why Most People Fail at Communication

Most people think they are good communicators. They
talk. They express. They share ideas.

But they don't connect. They don't persuade. They don't make people feel something.

The best communicators don't just deliver information—they control how that information is experienced. They make people believe in something bigger than themselves.

Because at its core, communication is not about words. It's about emotion. The world doesn't buy products. It buys the way products make them feel. No one spends six figures on a sports car because they need transportation. They buy it for status, power, admiration.

The best speakers in the world understand this. They don't just speak—they command attention. They create certainty. They reframe reality with their words.

And no one did this more powerfully in history than Winston Churchill.

The Speech That Changed a Nation

In 1940, Britain stood on the edge of destruction.

Nazi Germany had swept across Europe. France had fallen. The Luftwaffe prepared to bomb Britain into

submission. Fear spread like wildfire. The people were exhausted, terrified, ready to give up.

And then Churchill spoke. His voice carried the weight of an entire nation, but his words were unshakable.

"We shall fight on the beaches. We shall fight on the landing grounds. We shall fight in the fields and in the streets. We shall fight in the hills. We shall never surrender."

He didn't just tell them to fight.

He made them believe they could.

His words didn't just inform—they ignited.

With that speech, Churchill did what no military strategy, no political move, no defense plan could have done alone. He shifted the entire energy of a nation.

Britain didn't surrender. The people didn't break. They stood taller. They pushed forward. And against all odds, they held the line until the tide of war turned in their favor.

That is the real power of communication. The ability to make people believe in something greater than their fear.

The ability to turn hesitation into action, doubt into conviction, uncertainty into unstoppable force.

It is not intelligence, money, or experience that makes a person powerful. It is their ability to communicate in a way that bends reality to their will.

Mastering the Energy of Influence

The difference between an average communicator and a high-level influencer is not in their vocabulary, their grammar, or their facts.

It's in their energy. Most people talk. But great communicators pull people in.

They control tonality, shifting their voice at key moments—slowing down to build anticipation, speeding up to create urgency, using silence to make their words land harder.

They frame conversations in ways that make objections dissolve before they're even spoken.

They use stories, not facts, because they know that logic makes people think, but stories make people feel.

They know that certainty is more powerful than truth. People don't follow those who are the most correct— they follow those who are the most confident.

And once you understand this, you control every room you walk into. Because influence isn't about what you say. It's about how people experience what you say.

Are You Just Talking, or Are You Commanding?

Most people talk every day. But how many actually communicate?

How many people speak in a way that demands attention? That makes others stop, listen, and truly believe?

Look at the most successful people in the world. They aren't just intelligent. They aren't just skilled. They know how to sell themselves, their ideas, their vision.

Jobs and promotions don't go to the most qualified. They go to the person who communicates the best.

Businesses don't grow because of good products alone. They grow because of leaders who can persuade, inspire, and move people into action.

Relationships don't thrive on love alone. They thrive when people feel heard, understood, and emotionally connected.

Communication is not a soft skill. It is the ultimate power move.

Because when you can speak in a way that creates certainty, you become unstoppable.

So, the real question is: Are you learning to use communication as a weapon? Or are you just talking?

Because no one is coming to save you.

But if you master communication, you won't need saving.

Chapter 14

The Power of Relationships – Your Greatest Asset

The Power of Relationships – Your Greatest Asset

There is a force more powerful than talent, intelligence, or hard work—relationships.

They shape every opportunity, every door that opens or remains closed, every moment where success is either accelerated or denied.

You can be the most talented person in the room, but if no one knows your name, if no one believes in you, if no one vouches for you, **you will remain unseen**.

This is the reality most people ignore. They work themselves to exhaustion, believing that talent and effort alone will carry them to the top. But success doesn't operate in isolation. It moves through connections, through alliances, through the people who speak your name when you aren't in the room.

Look around at the most successful individuals in any industry. They aren't just skilled. **They are connected**.

And yet, most people misunderstand the nature of real relationships. They assume networking means collecting business cards, shaking hands, sending LinkedIn messages, but these surface-level interactions rarely change lives. What changes lives are deep, powerful, high-value relationships.

Think about where you are right now. Your job. Your finances. Your opportunities.

Now ask yourself: How much of this was influenced by the relationships you've built?

Did you land your job because of your résumé, or because someone introduced you to the right person?

Has your career growth stalled because no one in power sees your value? Do you find yourself constantly working harder but feeling unnoticed?

**Take a moment and really think. Are your
relationships working for you, or are they holding you
back?**

And it's not just about your career. Let's go deeper.

Think about your personal life. Your spouse, your
partner, your closest friends.

Do they push you forward, or do they keep you in place?
Do they inspire you, or do they drain your energy?

Are they helping you grow, or are they reinforcing your
limitations?

If you are with a partner who discourages your ambition,
constantly makes you question your worth, or doesn't
believe in your vision, **that is a relationship that is
actively working against you**.

If your closest friends don't challenge you to level up, if
they accept mediocrity, if they mock your goals instead
of pushing you toward them, then they are keeping you
stuck.

And let's talk about your boss.

Does your boss see your potential, invest in your growth,
and open doors for you? Or do they keep you in the same
role year after year, treating you as just another
replaceable worker?

Does your boss advocate for your success, or are they only focused on their own?

Because the truth is, if the person who controls your income doesn't respect you, see your value, or want to help you grow, you are putting your financial future in the hands of someone who has no intention of elevating you.

Now, let's be brutally honest.

If your spouse, your friends, your boss, your colleagues, and your inner circle are not actively elevating your life, what are they doing?

The relationships in your life are either an **asset or a liability.** They are either opening doors or locking them shut.

They are either **fueling** your **growth** or holding you hostage to the life you currently have.

And until you face this reality, until you audit your relationships with ruthless honesty, you will stay exactly where you are.

Success is not a solo journey. **No matter how independent you think you are**, no matter how much you believe in self-reliance, your ability to build and leverage relationships will define your future.

So, the question is: Are your relationships helping you win? Or are they ensuring that you stay stuck?

Why Relationships Matter More Than Talent

Imagine two people applying for the same high-level job at a prestigious company.

One is incredibly gifted with 10 qualified years of experience, a flawless resumé, and a deep knowledge of the industry. The other? Less experienced, less skilled, but happens to be the son of the CEO's best friend.

Who gets the job?

The one with the relationship.

Some people see this as unfair. But the truth is, success is rarely just about merit—it's about access.

Some are born into powerful circles. Others must build their way in.

And that's where most people fail. They spend years perfecting their craft, working tirelessly, believing that sheer effort alone will carry them to the top. But they never step into the right rooms. They never build the bridges that lead to game-changing opportunities.

Success isn't just about how good you are. It's about how connected you are. And no one understood this better than Cardinal Richelieu.

The Strategy of Building Power Through Relationships: The Rise of Cardinal Richelieu

History has shown that those who rise to the top do so not just through talent or ambition, but through **strategic relationships**.

No one embodied this more than **Armand Jean du Plessis, Cardinal Richelieu—a man who wasn't born to power, but built it from nothing**.

Born into a minor noble family in 1585, Richelieu should have been just another forgotten name in history—a bishop destined for a quiet life of religious service. But Richelieu saw something others didn't. He understood that power didn't belong to those with titles alone. **It belonged to those who could control the people who held the titles.**

From the beginning, he played the game differently. Instead of isolating himself in theological studies, he positioned himself where **decisions were being made**. He offered counsel to the right people, learned the desires of the most powerful figures in France, and most importantly, he made himself **indispensable**.

First, he gained the trust of **Queen Marie de Médicis**, acting as her advisor. This put him in proximity to the royal court, where he learned who **truly** controlled the kingdom. He identified the power players, the decision-makers, the gatekeepers of opportunity.

Once inside, he solidified his position. His ability to navigate conflicts, mediate political tensions, and offer **solutions when others only brought problems** made him respected. Respected men are heard. Trusted men are given power.

By the time he became Chief Minister to **King Louis XIII**, he **wasn't just an advisor—he was the true ruler of France**.

His power didn't come from his title alone. It came from **who he knew, who he influenced, and who relied on him**.

His lesson? **Your ability to build relationships will determine how high you rise.**

Positioning Yourself in the Right Circles

Most people struggle not because they lack talent, but **because they fail to position themselves where opportunities exist**. It's not enough to be good at what you do. If you aren't known by the right people, you'll always be overlooked. The most successful individuals **don't chase opportunities—they place themselves where opportunities naturally happen**.

They understand that the biggest deals, the most lucrative jobs, the most life-changing connections don't come from public job postings or cold outreach. They come from **conversations** behind closed doors, from **introductions made over dinner**, from friendships that turn into partnerships.

The reason some people effortlessly succeed while others struggle? They **understand the long game**.

They don't wait to be invited into rooms—they find ways to get in.

They don't approach powerful people asking for favors— they become so valuable that powerful people seek them out. And they never, ever let their relationships go cold.

The Long Game – Cementing Relationships for Life

Building relationships isn't just about meeting the right people—it's about keeping them in your life.

Most people make the mistake of only reaching out when they need something. That's not a relationship—that's a transaction. And powerful people don't invest in transactions.

The ones who win nurture their relationships. They check in. They offer value without expectation. They celebrate wins, show up when it matters, and build trust before they ever ask for anything.

Over time, this creates loyalty—the kind that opens doors money can't buy.

Protecting Your Reputation—Your Most Valuable Currency

The most valuable asset in business, in life, and in power isn't money. It's your name.

Your reputation will open doors—or shut them forever.

People trust those who follow through, who deliver, who make things happen without excuses. And in a world where everyone is trying to get ahead, trust is the most valuable currency of all.

The most successful individuals guard their reputation at all costs.

They only make introductions when it benefits both sides.

They don't speak in empty promises.

They ensure that when their name is mentioned in a room full of opportunity, it's followed by respect.

Because when people trust your name, they will fight to open doors for you.

How to Build *Relationships That Create Opportunities*

Relationships are not just about knowing the right people—they are about **becoming the right person in the right circles**. The difference between those who move through life with ease, finding opportunities at every turn, and those who constantly struggle to get ahead isn't luck. It's positioning. It's understanding that opportunities don't just appear—they are created through **relationships that matter**.

Most people misunderstand networking. They attend events, shake hands, exchange pleasantries, and collect business cards as if success is a numbers game. But the truth is, relationships that **actually lead to life-changing**

opportunities are built differently. They are based on **value, trust, and consistent presence**.

Too often, people make the mistake of approaching relationships with a taker's mentality. They meet someone influential and immediately start asking for favors, introductions, or business deals. They assume that just because they had a conversation, they are now entitled to help. But the most successful people don't operate this way. High-level individuals don't invest in relationships that drain them—they invest in relationships that **add value** to their lives.

The first rule of building meaningful connections is understanding that **you must give before you ever ask**. People naturally trust and remember those who bring something useful to the table. Instead of looking at someone as a potential resource, the better approach is to ask, how can I make myself valuable to this person? The most powerful individuals have goals, challenges, and projects that demand their attention. Those who help them move forward in those areas become the people they remember.

A young entrepreneur trying to break into the venture capital world might assume the best approach is to send an email asking for advice. But the one who makes an impact is the one who spends time researching an investor's latest project, providing insight they hadn't considered, or connecting them with someone valuable. This is the mindset shift that turns a **cold introduction into a lasting relationship**.

Beyond just offering value, relationships are built through **consistent presence**. Too many people let connections fade, only reaching out when they need something. But the most successful individuals understand the importance of staying visible and engaged. The key to maintaining relationships isn't constant conversation—it's **strategic, thoughtful interactions over time**. The occasional message to check in, a shared article relevant to their business, a genuine congratulations when they achieve something—all of these keep a relationship alive.

Powerful people naturally bring opportunities to those they **see regularly and trust deeply**. But trust isn't built overnight. It develops when someone proves their reliability over time. The fastest way to lose an opportunity is to **be inconsistent, unreliable, or only transactional**. If someone only hears from you when you need something, they will see you as **a burden, not a resource**.

Beyond staying in touch, positioning matters. If you want to build the right relationships, you must **be present where high-value conversations happen**. Success doesn't happen in isolation—it is cultivated in spaces where decisions are made. The best opportunities aren't

advertised publicly; they exist in **private conversations, exclusive gatherings, and behind closed doors**.

Those who succeed are not just meeting successful people by chance. They **intentionally place themselves in rooms where real discussions happen**. The biggest business deals aren't made in corporate meetings but over dinners, casual meetups, and events where decision-makers gather. The person who consistently shows up in these spaces, who listens, learns, and adds insight without forcing their way in, will find themselves naturally welcomed into powerful circles.

But there's a difference between **access and recognition**. Being in the same room as powerful people does not mean you are automatically one of them. Many make the mistake of entering high-level spaces and treating the people there as celebrities rather than peers. But successful individuals are not looking for fans—they are looking for equals. Those who act as though they belong, who engage in conversations with confidence rather than admiration, earn respect.

A person who walks into a private mastermind or an industry event and carries themselves with **certainty, presence, and intelligence** will command attention.

Those who hesitate, shrink in conversations, or position themselves as outsiders will be treated as such. Confidence in how you carry yourself, the way you speak, and how you contribute to discussions determines how people perceive you.

Once relationships are built, protecting them becomes even more important. In elite circles, reputation is **everything**. The fastest way to lose trust is to be **unreliable, make promises you don't keep, or push too hard for personal gain**.

Trust is what allows people to introduce you to their most valuable contacts, open doors that would otherwise remain closed, and extend opportunities that others will never hear about. The most respected individuals are those who protect their name, honor their word, and understand that relationships are **long-term investments, not short-term transactions**.

Everything in business, in influence, and in success flows through **who trusts you, who respects you, and who wants to see you win**. And trust isn't built through luck. It's built through **showing up, adding value, proving reliability, and playing the long game**.

If you want more opportunities, look at your relationships. Are you positioning yourself where success happens? Are you building relationships that open doors? Are you seen as an asset or an afterthought?

The Long Game – Cementing Relationships for Life

Building relationships is easy. Maintaining them for life? That's where most people fail.

A relationship is not a one-time transaction. It is a living, breathing connection that either grows stronger with time or fades into irrelevance. Too many people believe that simply knowing someone is enough, that a single meeting or a few interactions will keep the door open indefinitely. But relationships—especially the ones that truly matter—are **not self-sustaining**. They must be nurtured.

Think of every great relationship as an **investment account**. The more deposits you make—through value, trust, support, and engagement—the greater the return when you need it. But if you only withdraw, if you only reach out when you need something, if you never nurture the relationship, you will find the account **empty when it matters most**.

The most successful people understand this. They don't just build relationships—they **cement them over time**.

They know that the real value of a connection isn't in **the first interaction but in what comes afterward**.

People are quick to connect but slow to maintain. They attend a networking event, have a great conversation with someone powerful, and then disappear. They assume that because the interaction went well, the door will always be open. But in reality, **people forget fast**. Life moves quickly. Without consistent touchpoints, even the strongest introductions **fade into the background**.

This is why follow-up is everything.

Successful individuals don't wait months or years to reconnect when they need something. They **check in, stay visible, and remain engaged—without an agenda**. They make sure they are always **top of mind** so that when an opportunity arises, they are the first person remembered.

The key is consistency. Not in an overbearing way, not in a desperate way, but in **a natural, authentic way**. The best relationships don't feel forced—they feel like a constant presence, an unshakable familiarity.

A simple check-in, a congratulations on a major achievement, a casual message sharing an article that might be of interest—these moments add up over time. They create **a sense of continuity**, a feeling that you are **part of someone's world rather than just an occasional visitor**.

But cementing relationships isn't just about presence—it's also about **trust**.

The fastest way to ruin a relationship is to be **unreliable**. If you say you're going to do something, do it. If you offer to make an introduction, follow through. If you commit to a project, see it to completion. People in power don't have time for empty promises.

They don't have patience for inconsistency. The moment they sense that you are unreliable, that you don't follow through, that you overpromise and underdeliver, **you become a liability instead of an asset**.

And liabilities are quickly cut off.

The relationships that stand the test of time are built on **mutual respect and trust**. The ones who stay in the room, who are invited back again and again, who receive the most valuable introductions, are the ones who have **proven themselves dependable**.

The longer a relationship lasts, the deeper the **level of access**.

In the beginning, introductions might be casual, opportunities might be small, but over time, as trust is reinforced, **doors that were once locked start to open wider and wider**.

This is the long game.

The best deals, the highest-level partnerships, the most life-changing opportunities rarely happen in the first year of knowing someone. They happen **years down the road**, when the relationship has reached a level of comfort and trust so strong that people will bet **millions on your word alone**.

But only if you've played the game right.

The mistake most people make is thinking **too short-term**. They want results now. They meet someone powerful and immediately try to extract value. They push too hard, too soon, and burn the bridge before it was ever built.

Real relationships are **not about speed**—they are about **depth**.

A connection made today could become **the defining factor in your success ten years from now**. A person you help today, without expecting anything in return, could be the one who changes your life a decade later. The investor you meet at a conference but stay in touch with casually over the years could be the one who funds your company when the time is right.

You never know when the moment will come. But if you've done the work, if you've nurtured the connection, if you've built trust over time—when the opportunity presents itself, you won't have to ask.

They will offer.

That is the power of cementing relationships for life.

Chapter 15

The Art of Influence – Mastering the Power of Persuasion

Influence is Everything

Imagine stepping into a room where decisions are made—**big decisions**. The kind that can change your life, open doors, and create opportunities you never thought possible. You don't have the most money. You don't

have the highest title. You don't have decades of experience.

And yet, by the end of that conversation, everyone is nodding in agreement. They're sold. Not because you forced them. Not because you tricked them. But because you understood them. **You made them feel seen, heard, and understood in a way no one else did**.

That's influence.

And in the real world, influence is more powerful than money, titles, or **experience**.

If you can **master the ability to sway opinions**, to inspire action, to position yourself as the person who holds the answers, then you will never be at the mercy of circumstances again. You'll create your own luck. You'll generate opportunities out of thin air. You'll turn skeptics into believers, strangers into allies, and closed doors into open ones.

Without influence, you're just another voice in the crowd, hoping someone notices your value. And let me tell you the truth—**hope is a terrible strategy.**

Influence is Not Manipulation. Some people hear the word "**influence**" and immediately think of manipulation, deception, or mind games. But real influence isn't about controlling people—it's about understanding them.

People don't make decisions based on logic alone. **They are driven by emotion**, shaped by their fears, desires, and personal experiences. Influence is the ability to recognize what truly moves people and guide them toward a decision that benefits both of you.

When you influence someone, you're not forcing them. You're showing them a path they already wanted to take, but maybe didn't know how to get there.

Think about the most charismatic leaders, the people who walk into a room and command attention without demanding it. They don't manipulate. They connect.

They create a gravitational pull, drawing people in because they radiate certainty, clarity, and purpose.

Influence is about positioning yourself as the solution. The answer. The person who can help others get what they want.

Master that, and you'll never be overlooked again.

Influence Determines Who Wins

Every single major decision—whether in business, politics, relationships, or daily life—is influenced by someone.

The best product doesn't always win. The best-marketed product does.

The smartest person doesn't always get the promotion. The most persuasive person does.

The most talented artist doesn't always sell the most work. The one who builds the strongest connections does.

That's why you see mediocre politicians rise to power, average businesses dominate industries, and lesser-skilled people land dream opportunities—because they understand how to position themselves as the obvious choice.

But here's the truth: influence isn't reserved for the naturally charismatic. It's not something you're born with or something only extroverts possess. It's a skill. And just like any skill, it can be studied, refined, and mastered.

This chapter is about more than persuasion—it's about power. Not the kind of power that controls, but the kind that creates. The kind that allows you to shape your own future instead of being shaped by others.

Are you ready to master it?

The Science Behind Influence

To master influence, you must first understand one fundamental truth:

People do not make decisions based on logic alone.

If they did, the world would look completely different. No one would overspend on products they don't need. No one would stay in toxic relationships. No one would fear taking necessary risks to change their lives.

But human beings are emotional creatures. **We feel first, then justify with logic.**

This is why you can present someone with **all the facts, all the evidence, all the reasons they should say yes—** and they still won't budge. Because facts don't move people. **Feelings do.**

Think about the last time you made a big decision— buying a car, choosing a job, making an investment. Did you go purely off data, or was there something deeper at play? Maybe you had a gut feeling. Maybe you resonated with the salesperson. Maybe you felt like it was the right move, even before you could fully explain why.

That's how influence works. It taps into the **unspoken desires, fears, and motivations** that drive people's choices.

And while influence can seem like a mystical talent only a few possess, the truth is, there's **a science behind it.**

The Six Psychological Triggers of Influence

Psychologists and behavioral experts have spent decades studying what makes people say "yes." And while every situation is different, there are six **universal** triggers that determine how we make decisions.

Once you understand these, you'll start to see them everywhere—marketing, sales, leadership, relationships, politics, even daily conversations.

1. Reciprocity – Give, and you shall receive.

People feel a natural obligation to return favors. If you give value first—whether it's a compliment, a small favor, or an opportunity—people will instinctively want to give back. That's why companies give out free samples. That's why great networkers always help others before asking for anything. The more you give, the more people want to reciprocate.

2. Commitment and Consistency – Small steps lead to big decisions.

Once someone takes a small step in your direction, they are more likely to follow through with bigger commitments. It's why brands offer free trials—they know that once you start using the product, you'll feel compelled to continue. If you can get someone to say "yes" to something small, you increase the chances of them saying "yes" to something bigger later.

3. Social Proof – People follow the crowd.

Humans are wired to look to others for cues on how to act. If we see a restaurant with a long line, we assume the food must be good. If a product has thousands of five-star reviews, we trust it. If everyone in a room laughs at a joke, we're more likely to laugh too. The more people vouch for you, the easier it is to gain trust and influence others.

4. Liking – People say yes to those they like and trust.

We are far more likely to be influenced by people we genuinely like. And what makes us like someone? **Similarity, authenticity, and warmth.** If you can build real connections—by listening, showing empathy, and finding common ground—your influence will skyrocket.

5. Authority – People respect and follow experts.

Think about why we trust doctors, lawyers, or professors without question. The appearance of expertise carries weight. Even something as simple as dressing well, speaking confidently, or having credentials can increase your authority. If you position yourself as an expert in your field, people will naturally listen to you.

6. Scarcity – The less available something is, the more people want it.

Why do people scramble to buy limited edition sneakers or rush to book flights during "last chance" sales? Because when something feels rare or exclusive, its perceived value increases. If you make your time, skills, or offers feel limited, people will want them more.

Applying These Triggers in the Real World

These aren't just theories. They shape every business deal, negotiation, and relationship. Look at the most successful brands, leaders, and influencers, and you'll see these principles in action.

- **Apple uses scarcity** by creating demand through limited product launches.

- **Oprah builds trust and liking** by making deep emotional connections with her audience.

- Tesla **leverages social proof and authority** to make people feel like they're part of an elite group.

The key is not to memorize these principles, but to internalize them. Start paying attention to how you respond to influence in your own life. Notice when these triggers make you say yes—and then think about how you can use them **ethically** to create more opportunities for yourself.

Because influence is not about manipulation. It's about **understanding human behavior** and using that knowledge to build connections, inspire action, and open doors.

How a Man Used Influence to Build an Empire: Napoleon's Rise to Power

It was the winter of 1795. Paris was restless. The French Revolution had left the country in a state of chaos— bloody, divided, and desperate for stability. The streets were filled with angry mobs, riots erupted daily, and the government—known as the Directory—was barely holding on.

France didn't just need a leader. It needed a **savior**. And then came a young, ambitious general named **Napoleon Bonaparte**.

At the time, Napoleon wasn't a powerful man. He wasn't from a wealthy family. He had no high-ranking political connections. In fact, he was still relatively unknown in Paris. But what he **did** have was influence.

And he used it to change history.

The Moment That Changed Everything

The turning point came on **October 5, 1795**. A massive royalist uprising threatened to overthrow the government. The Directory was desperate—they needed someone to put down the rebellion before they lost control entirely.

Napoleon saw his opportunity.

He was put in charge of defending the government. But instead of hesitating or negotiating, he made a **ruthless, strategic decision**—he ordered his men to load **cannons with grapeshot**, a deadly spray of metal balls.

As the mob surged forward, Napoleon gave the order to fire.

Within **minutes**, the streets were littered with bodies. The rebellion was crushed. The government was saved.

And Napoleon became a **hero** overnight.

That one decision didn't just win him a battle—it gave him **influence over an entire nation**. The people saw him as the only man capable of restoring order. The Directory rewarded him by giving him command of the **Army of Italy**, a position that allowed him to rise even further.

But military power alone wasn't enough. Napoleon knew that **true power came from influence, not just force**.

Controlling the Narrative

Napoleon wasn't just a brilliant general—he was a **master of perception**. He understood that **influence isn't about what you do; it's about what people believe you've done**.

Every time he won a battle; he made sure the public **heard about it first—and in the most flattering way possible**. He controlled the newspapers, shaped public opinion, and made himself look like an unstoppable force.

He didn't just let history be written. **He wrote it himself.** By the time he returned to Paris in **1799**, he wasn't just a general. He was a legend. People believed he was the only one who could save France.

And that's when he made his boldest move yet.

The Coup That Changed History

In November 1799, Napoleon orchestrated a **coup d'état**, overthrowing the government and declaring himself **First Consul of France**.

He didn't take power.

He influenced people into giving it to him.

And just five years later, in **1804**, he took things even further. He **crowned himself Emperor**, refusing to let the Pope place the crown on his head. It was a symbolic act—he was showing the world that **his power didn't come from the church, the government, or tradition. It came from him.**

By mastering influence, Napoleon **rose from an unknown soldier to the ruler of an empire**.

The Key Lessons from Napoleon's Influence

Napoleon's rise wasn't about luck. It was about strategy.

1. He created value before demanding power.

Before he asked for anything, he **proved** his worth. He saved the government. He won battles. He established himself as someone people needed before he ever made a move for control.

2. He controlled the story.

Napoleon understood that perception **is reality**. He made sure people saw him as **the only solution**, and once they believed that, his rise was inevitable.

3. He positioned himself as a leader before he had the title.

Long before he was Emperor, he acted like one. He carried himself with **confidence, authority, and certainty**. The world followed him because he made them believe he was worth following.

That's the power of influence.

Napoleon didn't take control of France with brute force alone.

He influenced people to hand him the crown.
Modern Masters of Influence

Influence isn't just about war and politics. It defines **business, media, culture**, and even the choices you make daily—whether you realize it or not.

The people who shape the world don't necessarily have the most money, the best products, or even the highest intelligence. **They have the ability to make you believe in their vision.**

Some of the most powerful figures in modern history didn't force their way to success. **They influenced their way there.**

Let's look at three masters of influence—people who used **psychology, storytelling, and positioning** to change entire industries and, in some cases, the world.

Steve Jobs – Selling a Vision, Not Just a Product

Steve Jobs was not an engineer. He didn't personally build the first Apple computers. But what he did **better than anyone else** was influence the world to believe in his vision.

The Power of Storytelling in Influence
In **2007**, when Jobs unveiled the first iPhone, he could have listed its features: touchscreen, internet browsing,

music player, phone. But he didn't. Instead, he told a **story**. He painted a picture of a world where people **no longer needed separate devices** for calls, music, and the internet. He **made people feel** like they were witnessing a revolution—like they had to be part of it.

Jobs understood that people don't buy products. **They buy identities. They buy movements.**

And he used influence to position Apple as **not just another tech company, but a brand that represented innovation, creativity, and rebellion against the status quo.**

That's why Apple isn't just a company—it's a **cult-like movement**.

Jobs didn't just sell computers. **He sold a future that people desperately wanted to be part of.**

Oprah Winfrey – The Power of Emotional Connection

Oprah didn't become a billionaire by just interviewing celebrities. She became a billionaire by **mastering emotional influence**.

Trust: The Ultimate Form of Influence

Her entire career was built on making people feel understood.

When she talked to guests, she didn't just ask questions—she made them feel **safe enough to be vulnerable**. She turned interviews into **confessions, into therapy sessions, into deeply human moments**.

This wasn't an accident. Oprah understood that people follow those they **trust**.

And because she built unshakable trust with her audience, her influence became **unstoppable**:

If Oprah recommended a book, it became a bestseller overnight.

If she endorsed a product, sales exploded.

When she spoke, people listened—not because they had to, but because they wanted to. Her influence wasn't about power. **It was about connection.**

And in a world where everyone is trying to sell something, **trust is the most valuable currency there is**.

Barack Obama – The Power of Persuasion
In **2008**, Barack Obama was a young senator with limited political experience.

Yet, within two years, he **influenced millions** to believe he was the future of the country.

How He Used Influence to Win the Presidency

Obama's campaign wasn't built on policy debates. It was built on **emotion**.

He spoke in a way that made people feel like they were part of something **bigger than themselves**. He didn't just talk about change—he made people **believe they were the ones creating it**.

His speeches weren't just political. **They were transformational.** And he used the principles of persuasion flawlessly:

What These Masters of Influence Teach

Steve Jobs, Oprah, and Obama all mastered **different forms of influence**—but they all followed the same fundamental principles:

1. **They understood human emotions.**

Jobs made people feel like they were part of a movement. Oprah made people feel understood. Obama made people feel hopeful.

2. **They Controlled Their Narrative.**

Jobs didn't just sell computers—he sold "thinking differently." Oprah didn't just interview guests—she built deep trust with her audience. Obama didn't just campaign—he created a movement.

3. **They Made Influence Their Superpower** influence. made Apple the most valuable company in the world. Influence made Oprah one of the most trusted public figures. Influence took a young senator and turned him into the President of the United States.

The lesson?
 If you master influence, **you control your future**.

And in the next section, we'll explore exactly how **you** can start applying these lessons to your own life.

Final Thoughts:

Influence is Your Superpower

If you master influence, **you will never be ignored again**. The world doesn't automatically reward talent. It rewards those who **know how to position themselves, communicate their value, and shape perception**. Think about the people you admire—the ones who command attention, who seem to make things happen effortlessly, who always seem to be in the right rooms with the right people.

That's not an accident. They didn't wait to be chosen. **They built influence.** And if you want to control your own future, **you must do the same**.

The Truth About Influence

Influence isn't about manipulation. It's not about tricking people or forcing your way into success.

It's about **understanding people**—what they need, what they fear, what they aspire to—and positioning yourself as the person who can help them get there.

When you have influence: **opportunities come to you instead of you chasing them. Your voice carries weight in any room you walk into.**

People trust you, follow you, and believe in you.

Without it? You're just another person **waiting**—hoping someone notices your value. And hope is not a strategy.

The difference between those who win and those who

stay stuck isn't intelligence, skill, or luck. **It's the ability to influence.**

Ask Yourself This:
Do you want to be the person who:

Waits for permission?

Hopes someone else gives them a chance?

Stays silent, watching others take the opportunities they wish they had?

Or do you want to be the person who:

- Commands **attention.**

- Shapes **their own future.**

- Builds **relationships that open doors.**

- Never **has to beg for an opportunity because opportunities come to them?**

Because **nobody is coming to save you.**
But if you master influence, **you won't need saving.**

The Road Ahead

At this point, you have a choice. You can close this book, feel inspired for a few hours, and go back to the life you had before.

Or you can take **everything you've learned** and start applying it—today, not tomorrow.

Because knowledge alone changes nothing.

Action does.

The greatest mistake you can make is **thinking you'll have time later**.

The truth is, later **never comes**.

There's no perfect moment to start. There's no magical day when fear disappears, and confidence suddenly arrives.

The only way to become influential, powerful, and unstoppable **is to start acting like it right now.**

Master Influence, Master Your Life

Influence is your superpower. With it, you can:

- **Turn strangers into allies.**

- **Transform ideas into movements.**

- **Make yourself impossible to ignore.**

Without it, you're at the mercy of luck, hoping the right people notice you, hoping the right opportunities fall into your lap.

That's not power.

Power is **taking control of your own narrative**. Power is **making people see your value without you begging for it**. Power is **never being overlooked again**.

So the final question is

Will you use this superpower—or will you let life happen to you?

Conclusion

The Truth That Sets You Free

If you've made it this far, you are no longer the same person who picked up this book.

You've been challenged. You've been forced to confront truths that many people avoid for their entire lives. You've had to look at yourself—not just who you are today, but who you could be if you stopped waiting for someone to rescue you.

And now, there's no going back. Because once you know the truth, you can never unknow it: **Nobody is coming to save you.**

You are your own rescue. You are your own answer. You are your own solution.

And that truth, while terrifying for some, is the most liberating thing you will ever realize.

Because it means that **everything you want is still within reach—but only if you decide to reach for it**.

The Hardest Part Is Yet to Come

Right now, you're at a crossroads. You've gained new knowledge, new insights, and new tools to transform your life.

But knowledge alone changes nothing.

The hardest part isn't understanding the truth—it's living by it.

There will come a moment—maybe a week from now, maybe a year from now—where you will be tested.

You will face a setback so crushing that it makes you question everything you've learned. You will hit a wall so strong that quitting will seem like the only option.

That moment is where most people fall.

They remember the lessons, but they **don't apply them**. They talk about change, but they **don't live it**. They let old fears, bad habits, and negative people pull them back into their old lives.

But you?
 You have a choice.

The Excuses End Here

No more waiting.
 No more blaming circumstances.
 No more hoping for a perfect moment.

Because the truth is, **life doesn't care about your excuses**.

It doesn't care if you're scared. It doesn't care if you don't feel ready. It doesn't care if things feel unfair.

The world will keep moving—with or without you.

And if you refuse to take control of your own life, someone else will.

Your boss. Your competition. Your fear. Your past.

Something will dictate your future. If it's not you, then who?

Your Future Is Your Responsibility

Nobody can predict what will happen in your life. But one thing is certain:

The way you respond is entirely up to you.

No matter what obstacles stand in your way...
No matter who doubted you in the past...
No matter how many times you've failed before...

The next move is yours. You can put this book on a shelf and tell yourself you'll apply it **someday**. Or you can make a decision **right now**—that the excuses end here.

That you will bet on yourself, no matter what.

That you will outwork the version of you who wants to stay small.

That you will **do whatever it takes** to create the life you want.

Because now you understand the truth: Nobody's coming to save you. But you **never needed them to**.

Final Call to Action: Prove It

You've absorbed the lessons. You've seen the examples. You've felt the challenge. But now it's time to **prove it.**

Do one thing **today**—not tomorrow, not next week—to show yourself that you are in control.

Make that phone call, start that project, have that difficult conversation, walk away from the thing that's been holding you back. Take action.

Because at the end of the day, **this isn't just a book.**

This is a wake-up call. This is your turning point.
This is the moment where everything changes—**if you're willing to step up.**

So, the only question left is:

What are you going to do about it?

NOBODY'S COMING TO SAVE YOU

www.ingramcontent.com/pod-product-compliance
Lightning Source LLC
LaVergne TN
LVHW051240080426
835513LV00016B/1697